Changing **1**
Tomorrow
Grades 4–5

Grades 4–5

Changing Tomorrow 1

Leadership Curriculum for High-Ability Elementary Students

Joyce VanTassel-Baska, Ed.D., & Linda D. Avery, Ph.D.

PRUFROCK PRESS INC.

WACO, TEXAS

Prufrock Press Inc.
P.O. Box 8813
Waco, TX 76714-8813
Phone: (800) 998-2208
Fax: (800) 240-0333
http://www.prufrock.com

Table of Contents

Part I
Introduction to the Unit

Introduction
and Overview of the Unit

Rationale

The current clarion call in education to prepare students for the 21st century is an incentive to rethink elements of the curriculum that will best serve the interests of academically gifted and talented learners. One important component of a well-rounded curriculum is the inclusion of a formalized leadership development initiative to ensure these young people acquire the knowledge and skills essential to assuming leadership roles and to practice the habits of mind that will enable them to apply these behaviors in a conscientious and compassionate way. Incorporating such instructional opportunities into the curriculum offerings takes both planning and practice.

Changing Tomorrow 1 is designed to draw on some of the most powerful ideas associated with the newest paradigm in leadership development and to help teachers incorporate this knowledge into their curricula for high-ability students at the elementary school level. Although all learners can benefit from the information and exercises included here, the pacing of the lessons, the emphasis on conceptual thinking skills, and the focus on independent biographical research are best targeted to the abilities and needs of the advanced learner.

The design of the unit incorporates three conceptual strands:

◎ *Biographical studies*: The unit uses the biographies of six leaders drawn from a cross-section of fields to showcase the abilities, skills, and mindsets correlated with leadership practice. These individual case studies can serve as role models for students. Diversity in gender and race was a factor in their selection as was the level of contribution each has made to date.

◎ *Generalizations about the concept of leadership*: Based on the Taba (1962) Model of Concept Development, the unit is built around eight generalizations about leadership. These generalizations were culled from the theoretical and research base on the construct. Although there are myriad generalizations that can be articulated, the authors crafted these eight with an eye toward their prevalence in the professional literature and their salience for the age of the target population. The generalizations are included in Handout 1.1: Generalizations About Leadership, which is found in Lesson 1.

◎ *Ideas and exercises adapted from contemporary leadership literature*: The unit incorporates ideas and activities that have been adapted from a variety of materials and training guides on how to teach leadership skills. These application exercises have been tailored to elementary high-ability students.

Unit and Lesson Structure

Changing Tomorrow 1 is composed of 10 lessons that address leadership skill development at the elementary level for gifted students in grades 4–5. Goals and outcomes for the unit focus on inspiring leadership behaviors, enhancing skills in communication and collaboration, understanding the breadth and complexity of the concept itself, and strengthening metacognitive development. The unit also includes a pre- and postassessment on the concept of leadership that can serve as the basis for measuring student learning gains and instructional effectiveness.

Appendix A contains the Teachers' Rap Sheets, which consist of completed Biographical Charts for each of the leaders studied. They are not intended for distribution to students as they are akin to answer keys, but they will streamline the teacher's preparation process. An annotated bibliography in Appendix B details the scholarship that underpins unit conceptualization, design, and content selection.

The instructional component of the unit is composed of 10 substantive lessons; most lessons are subdivided into four or five parts, resulting in about 35 hours of teaching time across the whole unit. Three of the lessons are overarching in scope. Lesson 1 focuses on the introduction of the concept of leadership itself and is constructivist in orientation. Lesson 9 gives a panel of experts the opportunity to dialogue with students about these big ideas and real-world applications. Lesson 10 includes a final synthesis that requires students to integrate information from the individual case studies and to prepare a leadership profile assessing their own leadership abilities at this stage of their development.

Six of the lessons are focused on biographical case studies, and each contains an application of a skill tied to a single generalization. Lesson 2 uses Walt Disney to examine the idea of vision. Lesson 3 focuses on Ben Carson and empathic listening, a skill drawn from the generalization on communication skills needed in leadership. Lesson 4 explores Amelia Earhart and risk taking. Lesson 5 investigates Bill Gates and motivation. Lesson 6 is an extension of Lesson 5 and requires students to critique a speech by Mr. Gates and then use some of the same techniques to draft and deliver a speech of their own. Lesson 7 examines the life of Clara Barton and the link between adversity and leadership. Lesson 8 centers on Tecumseh and the idea of legacy—how time and history impact and often redefine a leader's ultimate contribution.

Across the six biographical lessons, there are some common threads. Each lesson begins with the in-class amalgamation of biographical information from the independent research students have conducted as homework. Students are expected to complete a Biographical Chart for each leader studied that requires them to abstract, prioritize, and summarize information on their own. In Part I of the in-class portion of each biographical lesson, students work with the teacher to create a master chart to ensure that there is a common understanding of the important elements of the leader's life. Part II of each of these lessons uses questioning techniques that require students to analyze, evaluate, and synthesize information, linking the leader's biography to the concept of leadership. Part III of most lessons is an application of a task derived from one of the generalizations studied in the unit. Part IV is typically focused on metacognitive awareness, using journal writing or other task demands that encourage self-reflection on the person and ideas studied and how they relate to the students' own leadership potential and development. Each instructional lesson concludes with student handouts.

In addition to the instructional parts, most lessons contain Assessment, Homework, and Extensions sections. Many of the extensions can be substituted for in-class work or homework, but they are primarily designed for independent study for individual students or small clusters of students.

Technology Requirements

The unit relies heavily on student access to the Internet to do the biographical research, and some lessons require that videos from the Internet be shown to the class as a component of an instructional activity. Suggested websites are included as starting points for students to begin their Internet research; however, the teacher can select additional sites for students to use as he or she sees fit. The teacher will also need to reproduce the handouts in the unit for distribution to the students.

Adapting the Unit for Local Needs

Like a three-dimensional jigsaw puzzle, the pieces of this unit on leadership interlock to ensure that the goals and outcomes are well covered. However, in education one size does not fit all classrooms. In order to make adjustments that will best suit local school parameters, the authors recommend that teachers first read all 10 lessons. This will reveal how the parts of each lesson tie together and build upon one another as the unit progresses.

If adjustments are needed, here are some ideas for consideration:

◎ The biographical research can be done as an in-class activity. In most instances, this will add another period to the length of the whole lesson. In districts where home access to computers is limited and public libraries are not easily accessible, this adaptation would allow the unit to still be taught. If done as an in-class activity, the number of elements students have to document should be reduced from five to three.

◎ The task requirements for the completion of the Biographical Charts by students can be stratified. The preferred model is that all students complete all assigned elements in the Biographical Chart. If this is too time-consuming and/or too repetitive, students can take responsibility for different elements in the chart. All students should read or view all of the material assigned for the research, but the time allocated to documenting the knowledge regarding a leader's life story can be reduced with this approach.

◎ The unit is designed for consecutive sequencing in the curriculum, and Parts I and II of each lesson should be delivered back to back. However, in some lessons, there can be spacing between Parts II and III without great loss in instructional continuity.

◎ Journal writing, which is typically found in Part IV of the lessons, can be done as homework. Teachers can preselect the questions they wish students to explore.

Three Clarifications to Facilitate Unit Implementation

The authors offer three clarifications as a kind of "heads up" in implementing this unit:

◎ There is a section included on the Teachers' Rap Sheet that is omitted on the student's blank Biographical Chart for each leader studied. The section is called Lasting Impact and Contributions. In the set of questions provided in Part II of each of the biographical lessons, there is a question asking students to identify these for each leader studied. Students were not asked to document this information as part of the homework because the intent is to get them to think on their feet during class to respond to this prompt.

◎ The Internet research on the six leaders studied is the primary basis for homework in the unit. In order to help students budget their time for conducting this research, you may want to distribute the full list of leaders studied, the recommended websites, and the due dates for completion of the Biographical Charts at the end of the first class session. This will ensure that students have plenty of time to complete the homework before each new lesson is started.

◎ There is intentional overlap on some of the Internet sites to which students are directed; their rereading of biographical material is designed to reinforce it in their memory banks. Although students are not tested on these biographical details, they need to have a fairly comprehensive knowledge of each leader's life story in order to construct responses to the questions pondered in the in-class discussions and in journal entries.

Curriculum Framework:
Goals and Outcomes of *Changing Tomorrow 1*

The following are goals and outcomes of *Changing Tomorrow 1*.

1. To provide role models for young people that will inspire leadership by example as an encouragement to seek and fulfill leadership roles and responsibilities for themselves. Students will be able to:
   o conduct biographical research on leaders using the Internet,
   o identify and evaluate the characteristics and skills of various leaders, and
   o synthesize the factors that contribute to effective leadership, including the talent development process.

2. To develop skills in communication and collaboration to deepen student understanding of the complex demands and challenges of leadership. Students will be able to:
   o develop listening skills that promote their understanding of other perspectives,
   o articulate their ideas in written and oral form, and
   o work individually and in multiple group settings to carry out an agenda or execute a sophisticated task demand requiring more than one person's effort.

3. To understand the construct of leadership as it manifests within and across various fields of human endeavor. Students will be able to:
   o construct a definition of leadership,
   o elaborate on team-building and conflict resolution skills as dimensions of effective leadership, and
   o apply leadership knowledge and/or skills to real-world problem resolution.

4. To develop metacognitive skills that will strengthen leadership capacity-building. Students will be able to:
   o articulate the skill sets and habits of mind of past and present leaders,

○ create products that reflect an understanding of leadership expectations and/or apply and assess selected leadership skills in carrying out multilayered task demands, and

○ reflect on their own leadership strengths and weaknesses through the creation of a personal profile.

Alignment
of the *Changing Tomorrow* Series With National Standards

In any new curriculum endeavor for gifted learners, it is crucial to show how it responds to the national view of curriculum standards in relevant areas. The following alignment framework shows how the *Changing Tomorrow* units respond to the 2010 NAGC Pre-K–Grade 12 Gifted Education Programming Standards, 21st-century skills (Partnership for 21st Century Skills, 2011), and the Common Core State Standards for English Language Arts (National Governors Association Center for Best Practices & Council of Chief State School Officers, 2010).

Alignment to the NAGC Pre-K–Grade 12 Gifted Education Programming Standards in Curriculum and Assessment

The *Changing Tomorrow* units align to the NAGC Pre-K–Grade 12 Gifted Education Programming Standards in the following ways:

◎ *Scope and sequence development*: The *Changing Tomorrow* units offer a set of interrelated emphases/activities for use across grades 4–12, with a common format and within a key concept on leadership with interrelated generalizations.

◎ *Use of differentiation strategies*: The authors used the central differentiation strategies emphasized in the standards, including critical and creative thinking, problem solving, inquiry, research, and concept development.

◎ *Use of acceleration/advancement techniques, including performance pre- and postassessments, formative assessment, and portfolios*: The authors used all of these strategies as well as advanced research skills to ensure a high level of challenge for gifted and advanced students.

◎ *Adaptation or replacement of the core curriculum*: The project extends the Common Core State Standards by ensuring that gifted learners master them and then go beyond them in key ways. Some standards are mastered earlier (e.g., reading and language skills), while others are practiced at higher levels of skill and concept in these leadership units.

◎ *Use of culturally sensitive curriculum approaches leading to cultural competency*: The authors have employed international and American multicultural leaders to ensure that students have an appreciation for the contributions of different cultures to our world today.

◎ *Use of research-based materials*: The authors have included models and techniques found to be highly effective with gifted learners in enhancing critical thinking, text analysis, and persuasive writing. They have also used the questioning techniques found in Junior Great Books and the William and Mary language arts units, both research-based language arts programs used nationally with gifted learners.

◎ *Use of information technologies*: The authors have used biographical research as a central tool for learning in an online environment. They also suggest the use of visual media, computer technology, and multimedia in executing the learning activities developed.

◎ *Use of metacognitive strategies*: The authors have included activities where students use reflection, planning, monitoring, and assessing skills. Each activity includes a journal entry that presses students to reflect on their understanding of leadership.

◎ *Use of community resources*: The units include opportunities for students to learn from a panel of experts or to interview a person central to understanding some aspect of leadership.

◎ *Career development*: Biography is the central reading tool used by the authors for students to learn about an eminent person who has demonstrated leadership skills in a given domain.

◎ *Talent development in areas of aptitude and interest in various domains (cognitive, affective, aesthetic)*: The units present people who have succeeded in various domains of human endeavor. Activities provide multiple opportunities for students to explore domain-specific interests, such as writing, viewing, and oral expression, thus exercising multiple levels of skills in cognitive, affective, and aesthetic areas.

Alignment to 21st-Century Skills

The *Changing Tomorrow* units also include a major emphasis on key 21st-century skills in overall orientation, as well as key activities and assessments employed. Several of these skill sets overlap with the differentiation emphases discussed above in relation to the gifted education standards. The skills receiving major emphasis include:

- *Collaboration*: Students are encouraged to work in dyads and small groups of four to carry out the research activities, to discuss readings, and to organize information on biographical material.
- *Communication*: Students are encouraged to develop communication skills in written, oral, visual, and technological modes in a balanced format within each unit of study.
- *Critical thinking*: Students are provided with models of critical thought that are incorporated into classroom activities, questions, and assignments.
- *Creative thinking*: Students are provided with models of creative thinking that develop skills that support innovative thinking and problem solving.
- *Problem solving*: Students are engaged in real-world problem solving in each unit of study and learn the processes involved in such work.
- *Technology literacy*: Students use technology in multiple forms and formats to create generative products.
- *Information media literacy*: Students use multimedia to express ideas and project learning.
- *Cross-cultural skills*: Students read and discuss works and events representing the perspectives of different cultures. They have opportunities to analyze different perspectives on issues.
- *Social skills*: Students work in small groups and develop the tools of collaboration, communication, and working effectively with others on a common set of tasks.

Alignment to the Common Core State Standards for English Language Arts

In addition to the 21st-century skills listed above, there are other points of integration with important curriculum standards such as the Common Core State Standards (CCSS) for English Language Arts. The units draw deeply on nonfiction literature, predominantly biography, as a basis for biographical study. The units require students to cite textual evidence to support their ideas, to integrate information from multiple sources, and to develop and justify their claims made during in classroom discussion. There is also time dedicated to reflective writing, which helps students develop self-awareness, critical thinking, and intellectual curiosity. Because the standards call for a major emphasis on developing argument, the *Changing Tomorrow* units require gifted and advanced students to analyze data, claims, and warrants in the material they read and to develop arguments on specific issues of leadership based on multiple data sources. As such, the unit is well aligned with the new CCSS.

Part II

Pre- and Postassessments and Rubric

Instructions
for the Assessments

One way to help teachers measure both student learning gains and instructional effectiveness is to use a pre- and postassessment tool. In *Changing Tomorrow 1*, this assessment is based on the students' breadth of understanding of the elements of the concept of leadership using a concept mapping technique. The same testing prompt is used in both the pre- and posttesting process.

Teachers should administer the preassessment before students begin the unit. This may be done on the day before or first day of implementation. Similarly, the postassessment should be administered when the unit has concluded. It can be administered on either the last day of implementation or closely following the last day. The suggested time frame for completing the assessment is 15 minutes.

A rubric is provided to use in scoring the instrument. Teachers should use the preassessment as a basis for judging how much students already know about leadership. The postassessment should be used to judge conceptual growth in understanding leadership.

In addition to sharing the results of the changes in learning with the students themselves, the teacher may want to aggregate the gain scores across all students. If the unit is taught over multiple years to different groups of students, the teacher will have a basis for assessing any improvements in instructional effectiveness over time. The scoring of the instrument should also lead to insights about what students absorbed or failed to absorb as a result of their experience in the classroom.

Preassessment
on the Concept of Leadership

(15 minutes)

Create a concept map to illustrate your understanding of the concept of leadership as we begin this unit of study. Draw a circle and put the word leadership in the center. Then, draw connections to that circle that describe how you understand the concept. Make as many connections as you can and label them. Then, describe the nature of the connections you have drawn.

Are there other things you know about leadership that you have not put in the concept map? Please add them below.

Name: _____ Date: _____

Postassessment
on the Concept of Leadership

(15 minutes)

Create a concept map to illustrate your understanding of the concept of leadership as we end this unit of study. Draw a circle and put the word leadership in the center. Then, draw connections to that circle that describe how you understand the concept. Make as many connections as you can and label them. Then, describe the nature of the connections you have drawn.

Are there other things you know about leadership that you have not put in the concept map? Please add them below.

Changing Tomorrow 1, Grades 4–5 © Prufrock Press Inc.

19

Permission is granted to photocopy or reproduce this page for single classroom use only.

Rubric for Scoring
the Pre- and Postassessments
on the Concept of Leadership

Please score each student paper according to the following dimensions of the activity. The scale goes from a 4 (*high*) to a 1 (*low*).

1. Students make appropriate *numbers* of connections to the concept.			
1 (*1–2 given*)	2 (*3–4 given*)	3 (*5–7 given*)	4 (*at least 8 examples given*)

2. Students make different *types* of connections to the concept.			
1 (*only one type of connection is provided*)	2 (*two types are provided*)	3 (*three types are provided*)	4 (*four or more types are provided*)

3. Students provide an apt description of the aspect of the concept delineated or the relationship of the concept to its connection.			
1 (*only one apt description is provided*)	2 (*two apt descriptions are provided*)	3 (*three apt descriptions are provided*)	4 (*four or more apt descriptions are provided*)

4. For additional ideas contributed about leadership, students should receive one point each, raising their score totals in uneven ways.

Add all point totals from the above items together to arrive at a student score. The top score would be 12+, depending on the fourth item on the rubric.

Part III
Lessons

Lesson 1
Introduction to the Concept of Leadership

Instructional Purpose

- ◎ To introduce the concept of leadership
- ◎ To share unit generalizations

Materials Needed

- ◎ Chart paper
- ◎ Markers
- ◎ Handout 1.1: Generalizations About Leadership

Activities and Instructional Strategies

This lesson is constructivist in orientation, so teachers need to follow the script offered below when teaching it. Students need to come up with their own ideas about leadership as the unit begins.

Part I (50 minutes)

1. Place students in groups of 3–5 to complete the following activities:
   - o Ask students to name as many people as they can who are leaders in American society. They should try to list at least 25.
   - o Have students make their list on chart paper and share the examples by group. As each group adds new examples, the teacher should generate a master chart of names.
   - o Groups should then categorize the domains in which their lists of leaders have contributed.
   - o Ask students to share their categories by groups. Create a master list of the domains of leadership generated. Ask students why some categories have several leaders but others have so few.
   - o Ask: What are some examples of leadership qualities needed to perform in these domains? Discuss a few and write them on the master list.
   - o Have students list nonexamples (people who are not exemplary of leadership qualities). Once they are finished brainstorming, have the groups share their examples. Make a master list.

○ Ask: What do these people have in common? What qualities do you think keep them from being leaders? Discuss as a whole class.

○ Instruct the groups to generate 2–3 generalizations about leadership. Ask: How do these generalizations apply to all of your examples and none of your nonexamples?

○ Have students contribute their generalizations to the master chart. Do they all fit the people generated as examples?

Part II (1 period)

1. In their groups, ask students to review their list of generalizations, as well as the unit generalizations (Handout 1.1: Generalizations About Leadership), and do the following:

   ○ Indicate which ones from their list are similar to the ones found in the unit.

   ○ Decide which unit generalizations apply to examples of people the group generated.

   ○ Determine which generalizations do not fit the work done thus far.

   ○ Tell students that both sets of generalizations will guide their development of understanding the concept of leadership better as they explore it through reading the biographies of great Americans, both contemporary and from the past.

2. Now ask students to generate a list of leadership qualities that they consider important, based on their work. Have each group share its list and create a master list for reference during the unit.

3. Ask students to choose one quality of leadership and write a one-paragraph argument supporting its importance for all leaders to possess. (Allow 15 minutes for the writing activity.)

4. Ask students to share 3–5 examples orally. Have students begin a portfolio of their writing for use during the unit and include this piece as their first entry.

Assessment

Teachers should use the constructed work of students as the basis for judging their initial understanding of the concept of leadership.

Homework

Students should read the material at the following websites on Walt Disney, the first leader studied in the unit.

◎ Wikipedia (http://en.wikipedia.org/wiki/Walt_Disney)
◎ Just Disney.com (http://www.justdisney.com)
◎ Biography.com (http://www.biography.com/people/walt-disney-9275533)

They should be given a copy of Handout 2.1: Biographical Chart: Walt Disney, found in the next lesson, to help guide their reading and to use for taking notes. Students should be instructed to fill out each element in the Biographical Chart with four or five pieces of information about Mr. Disney drawn from the readings. Students must read all three of the biographical entries and select important facts to include on their charts.

Name: _____ Date: _____

Generalizations About Leadership

◎ Leadership requires vision—the ability to see beyond what is to what might be by bridging the present and the future.

◎ Leadership requires the ability to communicate effectively with multiple individuals and groups regarding new ideas and plans for implementation.

◎ Leadership is based in action and often requires risk taking.

◎ Leadership requires the ability to influence and motivate others through words and actions.

◎ Leadership requires perseverance in the face of challenges and hardships.

◎ Leadership creates legacies that are best understood after the passage of time.

◎ Leadership is highly dependent on the interplay of intellectual abilities, specific aptitudes and skills, and personality factors.

◎ Leadership has shared and unique features across fields.

Lesson 2
Walt Disney and Vision

Our heritage and ideals, our code and standards—the things we live by and teach our children—are preserved or diminished by how freely we exchange ideas and feelings.

—Walt Disney

Instructional Purpose

- To practice using the Internet to do biographical research
- To map the biographical data against key leadership factors
- To understand the role of vision in leadership

Materials Needed

- Handout 2.1: Biographical Chart: Walt Disney
- Handout 2.2: The Vision
- Handout 2.3: Which Group Should Get the Funding?
- Teachers' Rap Sheet on Walt Disney (see Appendix A)

Activities and Instructional Strategies

Part I (1–2 periods)

1. Check that the Biographical Chart for Walt Disney has been completed.
2. Have the whole class complete a master Biographical Chart by using a white board or overhead projector to compile the information gathered by students. The teacher should start by asking: When was Walt Disney born? Is he still alive? What did you discover about Walt Disney's early family background and created family structure? What did you discover about his education? Follow this format until the master chart has been completed enough to ensure that the students have a fairly in-depth profile of the individual. The teacher may choose to annotate or extend the information in the Biographical Chart by drawing on the data provided in the Teachers' Rap Sheet found in Appendix A. Students should embellish their own charts as the class session unfolds.
3. Because this is the first lesson involving student research using Internet sites, the teacher may prefer to use in-class time to have students conduct the biographical research. If this is done as an in-class activity, additional time should be allocated to carry out this part of the lesson before commencing with the compilation of information on the master chart. In

addition, the teacher may reduce the number of data points that students collect for each element from four or five to three to save time in documentation. Refer to the Homework section of the previous lesson to find the website references to give to the students.

4. An additional option for compressing time if doing the research as an in-class activity is to stratify the elements assigned to individual students for data collection. Students would still have to read of all the material, but they would only need to document the data points for the specific elements assigned to them.

Part II (1 period)

1. The teacher will engage students in a large-group discussion using the following questions:
   o In what ways was Walt Disney a leader?
   o To what extent did time, place, and circumstances impact his ability to become a leader?
   o What personal characteristics contributed to Walt Disney's ability to become an icon in the family entertainment industry, including animated films, wholesome television programming, and the creation of destination theme parks?
   o How would you describe the vision that Walt Disney had for the field of family entertainment?
   o What evidence is there of both initiative and risk taking in Walt Disney's profile?
   o What evidence is there of Walt Disney's ability to communicate effectively as a speaker, a writer, and a listener?
   o What were some of the obstacles Walt Disney faced in becoming a successful cartoonist and businessman? How did he overcome these obstacles?
   o What do you see as Walt Disney's lasting impact and contributions in the areas of film, television, and family entertainment?

2. Put this quotation by Walt Disney on the board: "Our heritage and ideals, our code and standards—the things we live by and teach our children—are preserved or diminished by how freely we exchange ideas and feelings." Ask students to prepare a portfolio entry explaining what he meant by this. How did Mr. Disney's own vision contribute to the heritage and ideals of our country as we know it?

Part III (1 period)

1. Write the following quotation by Walt Disney on the board and ask a student to read it aloud to the class: "If you can dream it, you can do it." Then ask the class which of the generalizations on leadership this quotation directly addresses and why. Although the quotation can be linked to all of the first five generalizations, wait until someone has linked it to the one on vision before moving forward with the lesson.

2. Tell students that they are going to come to a fuller understanding of the concept of vision in today's lesson. If the teacher has already defined the term, he or she should also reference that definition, but the unit so far has not formally defined this term for the students.

3. Prepare a mini-lecture sharing the following information with students:

   o Almost all people who have studied the concept of leadership have identified that having a vision or guiding purpose the leader is passionate about and being able to share it effectively with others is the primary ingredient. A vision is a picture in the mind's eye of what will be different in the future from today. The leader must be able to transform the vision from dreamlike fantasy into reality in order to bring his or her ideas to fruition. According to Bennis and Goldsmith (2003), leaders "get results because their visions are compelling and pull people toward them. Their intensity, coupled with determination, is magnetic. . . . they draw others in" (p. 119).

   o By definition, a vision is a little cloudy and is also very grand. Here are some criteria that can be used to determine if the vision is a powerful one:

     • A vision engages your heart and your spirit.
     • A vision taps into needs that people share.
     • A vision crystalizes what you and others are desirous of creating.
     • A vision focuses on something of value, not something trivial.
     • A vision gives meaning to your work and to the work of others even if one's role in addressing the vision is small and specific in scope.

   o Back in the early 1950s, there was no Disneyland or Disney World. There was no Sea World, Universal Studios, or Six Flags Great America. There were amusement parks that had rides like Ferris wheels and merry-go-rounds that kids could go on. There were traveling circuses with animal acts and carnivals that had games people could play to win prizes. There were museums with dioramas and displays but no interactive exhibits. Today, in large part due to Walt Disney, we have many more complex options for hands-on, experiential entertainment. Walt

Disney had a vision for a bigger and better amusement park based on the characters he had brought to life in his cartoons, films, and television shows. He created a theme park—a park built around the theme of Disney characters and story lines. Walt Disney's vision for what could be created for a new type of family entertainment was a turning point in the entertainment industry.

4. Tell students that you are going to give them 5 minutes to come up with an idea for a new theme park or playground. The idea does not have to be strictly for fun; it may or may not have an educational component if they so choose. Tell them to jot their idea down on a piece of paper.

5. After 5 minutes, group students into triads or groups of four and pass out Handout 2.2: The Vision. Go over the instructions with students. Give the groups 20–30 minutes to reach consensus on a group idea for a theme park or playground and to write a vision statement describing their idea.

6. Have a representative from each group read the statement aloud to the rest of the class. Have the students evaluate the vision statements using the checklist provided on Handout 2.3: Which Group Should Get the Funding? After students have tallied their scores on the groups' vision statements, ask how many students gave Group 1 the most points, how many gave Group 2 the most points, and so forth until all hands have gone up or all groups have been assessed. Compliment all of the groups on their work and point out at least one or two positive outcomes of the exercise or the students' work.

7. Debrief the exercise using the following questions:
   o How is the concept of a vision or a vision statement clearer to you now that you have gone through this exercise?
   o Did your group pick an idea that one of your members had written down, or did you come up with a new idea in the group as you discussed the individual ideas? Did "group think" make your idea better or not? In what way?
   o Did having the criteria for evaluating the vision statement in advance affect your decision-making process? How so?
   o Was it easy or hard for your group to reach consensus on the best idea for the theme park or playground? Why?

Part IV (1 period)

1. The teacher will allow 10–15 minutes for students to complete their journals using some or all of the following questions as prompts. These ques-

tions may be put on the board or can be made into a handout that is inserted into the students' journals.

- o What did you learn from the biographical study of Walt Disney that is useful or interesting in your understanding of leadership?
- o What did you learn about Walt Disney that surprised you or helped you understand yourself better?
- o Is Walt Disney a role model for you? Why or why not?
- o What did you learn about creating a vision statement by going through this lesson? How does a vision statement provide a bridge between the way things are and the way they can become?
- o How important is having a powerful vision and communicating it effectively in leadership?

2. Ask a few students to share their responses with the whole class.
3. As an alternative to an in-class activity, the teacher may assign this as part of the homework.

Assessment

The teacher should check to see that each student has completed the Biographical Chart on Walt Disney and include it in the student's portfolio. The teacher should monitor the small-group work in Part III of the lesson to be sure that everyone is fully engaged and on task. The teacher should verify that the journal entries in Part IV have also been completed.

Homework

Students are assigned responsibility for completing Handout 3.1: Biographical Chart: Ben Carson in preparation for the next class period. The three sites that students should be directed to for conducting this research are as follows:

- ◎ Biography.com (http://www.biography.com/people/ben-carson-475422)
- ◎ Wikipedia (http://en.wikipedia.org/wiki/Ben_Carson)
- ◎ Academy of Achievement (http://www.achievement.org/autodoc/page/car1bio-1)

In addition, students should be asked to view the 2-minute video clip on YouTube entitled *Dr. Ben Carson's Inspiring Words*.

Extensions

The following ideas are offered as substitutions for parts of the above lesson or as extensions for this lesson focusing on Walt Disney and the role of vision in leadership.

◎ For homework or extra credit, have each student design a ride, display, or game that would be included in the theme park or playground they have envisioned. They may draw a picture of it, create a picture using images from magazines or the computer, or create an actual scale model or replica of it. When these are completed, allow students class time to discuss and showcase their work.

◎ Have students view clips from a classic Disney full-length film such as *Snow White, Cinderella,* or *Pinocchio* and compare and contrast it with a more recent animated film from Pixar or an anime cartoon. Have them identify innovations they see in the medium and discuss their reactions to the changes over the years.

◎ Walt Disney said,

> A hundred years ago, Wagner conceived of a perfect and all-embracing art, combining music, drama, painting, and the dance, but in his wildest imagination he had no hint what infinite possibilities were to become commonplace through the invention of recording, radio, cinema and television. There already have been geniuses combining the arts in the mass-communications media, and they have already given us powerful new art forms. The future holds bright promise for those whose imaginations are trained to play on the vast orchestra of the art-in-combination. Such supermen will appear most certainly in those environments which provide contact with all the arts, but even those who devote themselves to a single phase of art will benefit from broadened horizons.

How does this statement apply to the computer age? Have students break into small groups to discuss some of the artists of today's electronic media who have benefitted from and contributed to "art-in-combination." Where is the next generation of technological innovations headed? Who among them wants to ride that bandwagon? What skills are needed to be successful in such an enterprise?

◎ Have students view the 2004 documentary, *Walt: The Man Behind the Myth,* and write an essay based on what it contributes to their understanding of leadership and the personal elements and situational factors that underscore it.

Name: _____ Date: _____

Biographical Chart: Walt Disney

Full Name: _____

Lifespan: _____

Early Family Background and Created Family Structure

_____

_____

_____

Personality Characteristics and Areas of Aptitude, Talent, and Interest

_____

_____

_____

Major Career/Professional Events and Accomplishments

_____

_____

_____

Personal Life Themes/Beliefs

_____

_____

_____

Selected Quotations

_____

_____

_____

Awards and Recognition

_____

_____

_____

_____

Name: _____ Date: _____

The Vision

You're in luck! A few businesspeople are in town today looking for ways to invest some of their extra money in a new theme park or playground for family entertainment. They don't have much time to make a decision, so come up with a good idea and make your description of it concise and your case strong. Be as creative as you can be. All the investors really need to see and hear is your vision statement. The real details like the cost, location, timeline, and blueprint will come later.

Instructions

After you are in your small groups, have each person share the idea he or she came up with for a new theme park or playground for family entertainment. Use one of the ideas presented or come up with a new idea that the group can agree upon as the basis for your vision statement.

Explain your theme park idea, give some details about it, and write a vision statement for your group's idea in the boxes on the next page. Use the lines below to make some notes as you fine-tune your thinking.

1. In a few words, what is the theme or gist of the new theme park or playground that is different from anything that has been created before?

   _____

   _____

   _____

   _____

2. Give some details that will expand upon or clarify your theme park/playground idea, such as:
   o Who is it for?
   o What kind of rides, games, or displays will it have?
   o Why is it needed or wanted by intended visitors?
   o What will its benefit be to society?

   _____

   _____

   _____

   _____

Theme
(Write the theme in a few words.)

Additional Information
(Write a paragraph expanding upon the theme.)

Vision Statement

Name: _____ Date: _____

Which Group Should Get the Funding?

As individuals, use the following score card to evaluate the vision statements presented by the groups. On a scale of 1 to 5, with 1 being the *lowest* rating you can give and 5 being the *highest* rating you can give for each item, rate the ideas of each group.

Criteria	Group 1	Group 2	Group 3	Group 4
The vision of this theme park excites me.				
The vision addresses needs I see.				
The vision is something I want to be part of making happen.				
The vision is worthy of the time and money it would take to build.				
The vision, if carried out as planned, will make a positive difference in the world.				
Total Points				

Criteria	Group 5	Group 6	Group 7	Group 8
The vision of this theme park excites me.				
The vision addresses needs I see.				
The vision is something I want to be part of making happen.				
The vision is worthy of the time and money it would take to build.				
The vision, if carried out as planned, will make a positive difference in the world.				
Total Points				

Changing Tomorrow 1, Grades 4–5 © Prufrock Press Inc.

Lesson 3
Ben Carson and Empathic Listening

Between the covers of those books, I could go anyplace, I could be anybody, I could do anything, and I began to learn how to use my imagination more . . .

—Ben Carson

Instructional Purpose

- ◎ To practice using the Internet to do biographical research
- ◎ To map biographical data against key leadership factors
- ◎ To understand the leadership skill of empathic listening

Materials Needed

- ◎ Handout 3.1: Biographical Chart: Ben Carson
- ◎ Handout 3.2: Practicing Empathic Listening Skills
- ◎ Teachers' Rap Sheet on Ben Carson (see Appendix A)

Activities and Instructional Strategies

Part I (1–2 periods)

1. The teacher will have the whole class complete a master Biographical Chart on Ben Carson, based on the information students found from completing their prior homework assignment research. This should be done using a white board or overhead projector, as was done in Lesson 2. Again, as in Lesson 2, the teacher should use questioning techniques to gather the data needed to complete a master chart. The teacher may choose to annotate the information collected by drawing on the Teachers' Rap Sheet for Dr. Carson if students have failed to grasp and/or record important pieces of biographical information.
2. Conclude this lesson by asking students to draw some comparisons and some contrasts between the life stories of Walt Disney and Ben Carson.

Part II (1 period)

1. The teacher will engage students in a large-group discussion using the following questions:
   - In what ways is Ben Carson a leader?

○ To what extent did time, place, and circumstances impact his ability to become a leader?

○ What personal characteristics contributed to Ben Carson's ability to become a successful brain surgeon and director of pediatric neurosurgery at one of the leading university hospitals in the world?

○ How would you describe the vision that Ben Carson had for the field of neurosurgery?

○ What evidence is there of both initiative and risk taking in Ben Carson's profile?

○ What evidence is there of Dr. Carson's ability to communicate effectively as a speaker, a writer, and a listener?

○ What were some of the obstacles Dr. Carson faced in becoming a successful brain surgeon? How did he overcome these obstacles?

○ What was the main message in the video clip you viewed and how does it relate to Dr. Carson's outlook on life?

○ What do you see as Ben Carson's lasting impact and contributions in the areas of medicine and philanthropy based on what you know at this time?

○ Ben Carson said, "There is no such person as a self-made individual." What do you think he means by this? How did other people influence and help the young Ben Carson in his talent development process?

2. Ask students to do a journal entry on one of the last two sets of questions above. (Allow 15 minutes.)
3. Have a few students share and discuss their responses.

Part III (1–2 periods)

1. The teacher will introduce this component of the lesson with a mini-lecture highlighting the following information as appropriate for the class.

> Effective communication is a core skill in motivating and inspiring others to participate in pursuing a vision. Stephen Covey (2004) has identified empathic communication as one of the key ingredients in the ability to understand others and to be understood by them. He believes that students receive much instruction in the skills of reading, writing, and speaking, but far less in the skill set of listening, which is often the primary vehicle for understanding the intentions or needs of other people. Empathic listening is listening with one's

ears, eyes, and heart. Much of our communication with each other is nonverbal. We communicate boredom with a yawn, amusement with a smile, sadness with a tear, and anger with a stony glare. Sometimes our words match our emotional expressions; sometimes our emotional expressions reveal that our words are not telling the whole truth of the matter. Empathic listening is more than reflecting back to the person what the person has said. Empathic listening is trying to see the world through the other person's eyes.

Ben Carson is a master of empathic listening. In deciding whether or not to do brain surgery on a patient, he must weigh the advantages and disadvantages (benefits and risks) of proceeding or not proceeding with the operation. In one case, he was asked to separate conjoined Iranian twins whose prognosis was highly guarded.

At first, Dr. Carson refused to perform the surgery, but when another surgical team in Singapore agreed to undertake the operation, Dr. Carson decided to assist. When interviewing the twins, both said they would rather die than spend another day stuck to each other. Dr. Carson tried to put himself in their shoes. What would it be like to be tied to another person for 24 hours a day every single day when that person had different aspirations and interests than you? The words of the twins and their feelings of frustration and sadness made Dr. Carson decide to participate on the team that tried to separate the twins. Although the operation was not successful, Dr. Carson took comfort in knowing that he had acted in accordance with the wishes of his patients.

2. After sharing the aforementioned information with students, the teacher should demonstrate to the class two statements that have emotional undertones. In one statement, the emotional expression should be consistent with the statement; in the other statement, there should be a disconnect between the words and the facial expression or body language. For example, with a smile on your face, say aloud, "I am really angry with you today." Ask the class if the words are consistent with the nonverbal cues. Then, with a smile on your face, say aloud, "I am very pleased with your interest in studying leadership." Again, ask the students if the words are consistent with the facial expression. Tell the class that they are going to practice empathic listening.

3. Divide the class into groups of four and pass out Handout 3.2: Practicing Empathic Listening Skills. Have the first person in each group tell about a time when he or she had a deep or vivid emotional experience. The student might pick a time when he or she was very happy, sad, angry, scared, or furious. The student should try to give details of the event or activity that triggered the feelings. The second student should repeat the incident or experience that the first person has described (reflecting back) using the same words or different words (paraphrasing) to restate it. The third person should describe a time when he or she had a similar feeling (sharing the feeling). The trigger or catalyst for the feeling might be very different, but the response to the trigger should be the same. If the first student has described a happy time, the third student must describe a happy time in his or her own life (again giving some details to the event). The fourth student should closely observe *what* both the first and third students have said and *how* they said it. The fourth student should assess whether or not the students who were telling about their past experiences were feeling the emotion that they were describing or whether they were now distanced from it (discussing it objectively, not subjectively). The fourth student should share his or her assessment with the group and explain how he or she came to that conclusion. The first and third students should confirm the accuracy or inaccuracy of this assessment and discuss any discrepancies. The second student should report what feelings he or she had, if any, when repeating the first student's experience.

4. Repeat the process at least once more, giving students an opportunity to change roles. If time allows, repeat the process a third time. With each round, have the students select a different feeling to work through.

5. Reconvene the whole class to discuss what observations students had about the experience. Questions to probe the student reflections include:
   o Were they comfortable or uncomfortable with the task?
   o Did the sharing of feelings with one another lead to more connectedness, or did it create more distance among them? Why did this happen?
   o Were the four roles equally easy to perform, or were some roles more challenging than others? Have students give examples and explain their answers.
   o Why was it useful to have multiple roles to practice empathic listening skills?
   o How important is empathic listening in being an effective leader?

Part IV (1 period)

1. The teacher will allow 10–15 minutes for students to complete their journals using some or all of the following questions as prompts. These questions may be put on the board or can be made into a handout that is inserted into the students' journals.
   o What did you learn from the biographical study of Ben Carson that is useful or interesting in your understanding of leadership?
   o What did you learn about Ben Carson that surprised you or helped you understand yourself better?
   o Is Ben Carson a role model for you? Why or why not?
   o What did you learn about communication skills by going through the exercise on empathic listening? Are you a good empathic listener? Why or why not?
   o How important is empathic listening in leadership?

2. The teacher should ask some students to share their responses with the whole group and explore some of the ideas presented.

Assessment

The teacher should check to see that each student has completed the Biographical Chart on Ben Carson. The teacher should monitor the small-group work in Part III of the lesson to be sure that everyone is fully engaged and on task. The teacher should verify that the journal entries have also been completed.

Homework

Students are assigned responsibility for completing Handout 4.1: Biographical Chart: Amelia Earhart in preparation for the next class period. The four sites that students should be directed to for conducting this research are as follows:
   ◎ Wikipedia (http://en.wikipedia.org/wiki/Amelia_Earhart)
   ◎ The Official Website of Amelia Earhart (http://ameliaearhart.com)
   ◎ Biography.com (http://www.biography.com/people/amelia-earhart-9283 280; the website includes a 42-minute video for optional viewing based on the teacher's preference)
   ◎ About.com (http://womenshistory.about.com/od/quotes/a/amelia_earhart.htm; this website contains examples of quotations by Amelia Earhart)

The teacher should remind students to read the material on all four of the websites even though they only have to document four or five examples of each element on the chart. As an option, the teacher may stratify the documentation requirements by assigning only selected elements to each student so that the chart can be completed in Part I of the next lesson by the class as a whole.

Extensions

The following ideas are offered as substitutions for parts of the above lesson or as extensions for this lesson focusing on Ben Carson and the role of communication in leadership.

- Have students view the video clip entitled *Ben Carson: An Extraordinary Life*, one of the conversations from Penn State that is available on YouTube (approximately an hour in length). The interview covers myriad topics including his personal background, his thoughts on healthcare funding policy, his philanthropy, his support systems, his interest in classical music, the human brain and its plasticity, risk taking and its consequences in medicine, his abandonment by his father, and the way he would like to be remembered. On an individual basis, have each student pick out a comment, observation, or idea that captured his or her interest during the interview and write a paragraph on how the comment, observation, or idea relates to or expands his or her understanding of leadership. (If you choose to do this as an in-class exercise, the segment on healthcare funding policy can be fast-forwarded as it will probably be difficult for students to relate to.)

- Ben Carson has said, "It does not matter where we come from or what we look like. If we use our abilities, are willing to learn and to use what we know in helping others, we will always have a place in the world." In dyads or small groups, have students discuss the following questions: What is your own vision for your career? What interests, skill sets, and/or abilities do you see in yourself at this stage of your life? What do you want or need to do to develop these skills or abilities into a job or career path that can make a difference in the world? Is being of help to others something that is important to you at this stage of your life? What other values besides that of being of service to others should someone take into account when deciding on a career choice?

- For independent work, encourage students to read *Gifted Hands, Kids Edition: The Ben Carson Story* by Gregg Lewis and Deborah Shaw Lewis. Instead of having students write a traditional book report, require an essay that describes at least three examples of Ben Carson's leadership potential as a child or leadership skills evident as a teen or adult that were presented in the book that were different from or significantly enriched and expanded the material available on the Internet research sites. Ask them to evaluate what characteristics they see in themselves that suggest current or future leadership abilities.

◎ For independent work, have students view the DVD of *Gifted Hands: The Ben Carson Story* starring Cuba Gooding, Jr. Have students each create a "Vision Board" of the goals young Ben might have dreamed about and the obstacles he had to overcome to achieve his goals. After students share their Vision Boards with classmates, ask them how making it requires a kind of empathic listening strategy (i.e., listening with your ears, eyes, and heart).

Handout 3.1

Biographical Chart: Ben Carson

Full Name: _____

Lifespan: _____

Early Family Background and Created Family Structure

_____

_____

_____

Personality Characteristics and Areas of Aptitude, Talent, and Interest

_____

_____

_____

Major Career/Professional Events and Accomplishments

_____

_____

_____

Personal Life Themes/Beliefs

_____

_____

_____

Selected Quotations

_____

_____

_____

Awards and Recognition

_____

_____

_____

Name: _____ Date: _____

Practicing Empathic Listening Skills

In this assignment, each student in the group will be performing one of four roles each time the exercise is done. As the exercise is repeated, students will switch roles and a different emotion will be used.

Roles

◎ **The Teller:** The teller starts the exercise by describing a time when he or she had a deep emotional experience. The teller can pick the kind of emotion that he or she is willing to share with the other members of the small group. It might be related to feelings of happiness, sadness, anger, fear, jealousy, or spite. The teller should try to give details of the event or activity that triggered the feeling he or she wants to describe. For instance, when it happened, who else was around, and the sights, sounds, smells, or other sensations that accompanied the feeling. The teller should also address the aftermath or consequence of having the feeling. If you are the teller, you may find that in talking about the emotional experience, you may reexperience the same feeling you had when it actually happened.

◎ **The Echo:** The echo is the second person to speak. He or she must have listened intently to what the teller has shared, and then should repeat the experience back to the group. The echo may use the same words or different words (paraphrase) to restate the teller's story. This is done to show the teller that his or her words have been heard.

◎ **The Mirror:** The mirror should describe a time when he or she had the same feeling that the teller had. If the teller describes a happy time, the mirror should also describe a happy time. Again, there should be details about the event or activity that caused the same feeling to occur. This is done to show the teller that the feelings connected to his or her words have been heard.

◎ **The Observer:** The observer listens intently to *what* both the teller and the mirror have said and observes *how* they said it. The observer's job is to assess whether or not the students who were the teller and the mirror were reexperiencing the emotion they were describing or were just reporting it. If the observer sees signs that the teller or the mirror were reexperiencing the same emotion as they related their stories, the observer should point out what these signs were.

After the observer has reported his or her observations and conclusions, the teller and the mirror can confirm whether or not the observer's assessment is accurate. The echo can then comment on what he or she was feeling, if anything, while repeating the teller's story.

Note: It is hard for some people to share their feelings with others. Please be respectful of the information that your fellow students are sharing and treat it with kindness and dignity.

Lesson 4
Amelia Earhart and Risk Taking

> *The most difficult thing is the decision to act, the rest is merely tenacity. The fears are paper tigers. You can do anything you decide to do. You can act to change and control your life; and the procedure, the process is its own reward.*
> —Amelia Earhart

Instructional Purpose

- ◎ To practice using the Internet to conduct biographical research
- ◎ To map biographical data against key leadership factors
- ◎ To learn about risk-assessment processes

Materials Needed

- ◎ Answer Key for Handout 4.2: Taking Calculated Risks
- ◎ Handout 4.1: Biographical Chart: Amelia Earhart
- ◎ Handout 4.2: Taking Calculated Risks
- ◎ Teachers' Rap Sheet on Amelia Earhart (see Appendix A)

Activities and Instructional Strategies

Part I (1–2 periods)

1. Amelia Earhart represents the second biography of a leader whose lifetime does not overlap in any way with students in the class or even with that of their parents. For this reason, the teacher may want to introduce this section of the lesson by pointing out a few important events that occurred in Ms. Earhart's lifetime:

   o In the late 1920s and through the 1930s, the country had its most severe economic depression in its history. Almost one in four adults could not find work.

   o In 1920, the 19th Amendment was passed, giving women the right to vote.

   o The Wright brothers invented the airplane in 1903; in 1914, the first commercial airplane flight was scheduled in the U.S.

   o In 1925, the Ford Motor Company constructed the first successful commercial plane, which carried 12 passengers.

   o After WWI, there were many trained pilots, so the aviation industry took off.

2. The teacher will break the students into triads or groups of four and have each group complete a master Biographical Chart by sharing the information collected on Amelia Earhart for homework. Upon completion of the full chart by each group, the teacher will reconvene the whole class to fill in any blanks or to correct any misunderstandings regarding the biographical details of Ms. Earhart's life. To start this process, the teacher will ask one of the small groups to share the information it compiled for the first two sections of the chart.

3. The teacher will then ask if anyone else in the class has information to add to these two sections of the chart.

4. Before going onto the next sections of the chart, ask: Do you have any questions about the information in these two sections of the chart? The teacher should use a parallel process and set of questions for the remaining sections on the chart. As in prior lessons, the teacher may choose to annotate or expand upon the information compiled by students by drawing on the Teachers' Rap Sheet for Ms. Earhart.

5. To conclude this part of the lesson, the teacher should ask students what profession Amelia Earhart might have pursued if she had been born in the 1950s or 1960s rather than in 1897.

Part II (1 period)

1. The teacher will engage students in a large-group discussion using the following questions:
   o In what ways was Amelia Earhart a leader?
   o To what extent did time, place, and circumstances impact her ability to become a leader?
   o What personal characteristics contributed to Amelia Earhart's ability to become a successful aviatrix and advocate for gender equality?
   o How would you describe the vision that Amelia Earhart had for the fledgling field of aviation? How has her vision come into full bloom in more modern times?
   o What evidence is there of both initiative and risk taking in Amelia Earhart's profile?
   o What evidence is there of Ms. Earhart's ability to communicate effectively as a speaker, a writer, and a listener?
   o What evidence do you see of Ms. Earhart's ability to motivate others?
   o What obstacles did Ms. Earhart encounter in her lifetime? How did she overcome them?
   o What do you see as Amelia Earhart's lasting impact and contributions to the areas of aviation and gender equality?

- o Amelia Earhart said, "The most difficult thing is the decision to act, the rest is merely tenacity. The fears are paper tigers. You can do anything you decide to do. You can act to change and control your life; and the procedure, the process is its own reward." What do you think she meant by this?

2. Ask students if they remember the main idea in the video clip they viewed from the Ben Carson lesson. Have one or two students comment on the message in the clip. Then ask students to write a response to this question: How is the quotation from Amelia Earhart similar to and different from the message in the Ben Carson video clip? Discuss their responses with the whole group.

Part III (1–2 periods)

1. Tell students that this part of the lesson focuses on the third generalization studied in this unit, the one dealing with leaders in action and the willingness to take risks. Ask students why they think that these two behaviors are linked together into one generalization. In other words, what is the relationship between initiating action and taking risks? Have more than one student comment on this relationship. Then ask students if taking risks is the same as being reckless. See if they can clarify the difference. (Recklessness requires risk taking, but risk taking does not require recklessness.) In fact, a competent leader is not reckless and must learn and use strategies for assessing risk and for managing risk to protect him- or herself and/or his or her organization from poorly considered decisions.

2. Remind students that they cited examples of initiative and risk taking in the profiles of Disney, Carson, and Earhart. Ask them to look across all three profiles and decide who took the greatest risks. By show of hands, ask students to indicate their choices. Ask for volunteers to explain their selections. If all students selected Earhart, play devil's advocate with Carson.

3. Distribute Handout 4.2: Taking Calculated Risks, and go over the main ideas with students. Risk requires three conditions:
   - o the potential for loss or gain (may involve opportunities, reputation, or even life),
   - o the likelihood of the occurrence, and
   - o the ability to make a choice that impacts the occurrence of the potential loss or gain.

4. Ask students if they can explain the difference between the terms *risk assessment* (a process for determining the conditions of risk resulting from an action or inaction) and *risk management* (a rational process for responding to a known risk or risks). Prompt students until they are able to make this distinction between the two terms. Then go over the section of the handout that identifies the four basic ways that risk can be treated:
   o avoidance (eliminate the risk, withdraw from the risk, or do not enter into the situation that presents the risk),
   o reduction (optimize the potential for a positive outcome or weaken the potential for a negative outcome),
   o sharing (transfer the risk elsewhere, redistribute the costs of the risk among parties, or purchase insurance against the risk), and
   o retention (accept the risk and plan for the costs associated with its occurrence).

5. Tell students to pretend that it's 1937, and they are in Amelia Earhart's shoes. Remind them that she is the most famous aviatrix in the world, with many successful flights under her belt. The technology of airplanes is constantly being improved although the industry is still in its early stages of development and commercial travel is not yet widely available or accepted. Remind them there are no cell phones or GPS devices invented yet (if this has not already come up in discussing her biography). She has no way of knowing what the actual outcome of her decision will be.

6. Have a student read the question on Handout 4.2: "Should I, Amelia Earhart, try to be the first woman to fly around the world?" Work with the whole class to complete the chart on the handout. An answer key for this chart is included at the end of this lesson.

7. After completing the chart as a whole group, ask students if there are other outcomes (potential losses or gains) between the best and worst cases that could be anticipated or considered. Have them name some of these outcomes (e.g., Earhart could have initiated the flight but not completed it due to weather problems; she could have initiated the flight but bailed out over the ocean and have been rescued at sea; her plane could have been damaged prior to takeoff, and she might have never undertaken the trip). Ask students if the same risk assessment process could be used on other potential outcomes.

8. Break the class into small groups of no more than five students per group, and have each group come up with a situation that hasn't yet happened and apply the risk assessment matrix to it (allow 15–20 minutes). The situation may be of local or regional interest (e.g., whether or not the class should go skydiving on their next field trip, whether or not the class

should sponsor a bake sale to raise money for school uniforms) or of national or international concern (e.g., whether or not the U.S. should reduce its nuclear arms capacity).

9. Ask for a volunteer from each group to report the results to the whole class. Clarify any misunderstandings or misperceptions of the risk assessment/risk management process. Debrief the exercise by asking the following questions:
   o How are the concepts of risk assessment and risk management clearer to you now that you have gone through this exercise?
   o How important are risk assessment and risk management in carrying out leadership responsibilities? How does an effective risk assessment/management process build trust between leaders and their followers?
   o Was it easy or hard for your group to reach consensus on the best situation to use to apply the matrix? Why?
   o Was there any conflict in your group in reaching a decision about the situation or in completing the matrix? Give an example of this conflict and tell how you worked through it.

Part IV (1 period)

1. The teacher will allow 10–15 minutes for students to complete their journals using some or all of the following questions as prompts. These questions may be put on the board or can be made into a handout that is inserted into the students' journals.
   o What did you learn from the biographical study of Amelia Earhart that is useful or interesting in your understanding of leadership?
   o What did you learn about Amelia Earhart that surprised you or helped you understand yourself better?
   o Is Amelia Earhart a role model for you? Why or why not?
   o What did you learn about risk taking by going through the exercise on risk assessment and risk management?
   o In order to be able to take risks, you must also be willing to fail or make mistakes. How do you handle failure in yourself? Are you tolerant or intolerant of failure in others?

2. Ask a few students to share their responses with the class.

Assessment

The teacher should check to see that each student has completed the Biographical Chart on Amelia Earhart. The teacher should monitor the small-group work in Part III of the lesson to be sure that everyone is fully engaged and on task. The teacher should insert the completed Handout 4.2 into each student's portfolio and should verify that the journal entries have also been completed.

Homework

Students are assigned responsibility for completing Handout 5.1: Biographical Chart: Bill Gates in preparation for the next class period. The four sites that students should be directed to for conducting this research are as follows:

- ◎ Wikipedia (http://en.wikipedia.org/wiki/Bill_Gates)
- ◎ The Official Site of Bill Gates (http://www.thegatesnotes.com)
- ◎ Microsoft Corporation (http://www.microsoft.com)
- ◎ BrainyQuote (http://www.brainyquote.com/quotes/authors/b/bill_gates.html)

The teacher should remind students that they must read the material on all four sites regarding Mr. Gates and to find four or five examples of data for each element on the Biographical Chart.

Extensions

The following ideas are offered as substitutions for parts of the above lesson or as extensions for this lesson focusing on Amelia Earhart and risk taking in leadership.

- ◎ Have students view the 42-minute video on Biography.com. Ask them to pick out some ideas or images from the film and discuss how these ideas or images amplified their knowledge of Amelia Earhart's life and times. This may be done as a discussion or as a written commentary. Ask students to also address how the film supported or changed their understanding of the risks that Earhart assumed in making aviation history.
- ◎ Amelia Earhart was an amateur poet and did not seek to publish her work. In small groups, have students ponder and discuss why she did not show much risk taking in sharing her poems but showed remarkable risk taking in her career in aviation. Ask students to think of other examples of leaders who are willing to take big risks in some aspects of their lives but are quite timid and restrained in other aspects of life. What can they derive or infer about risk taking from examining examples of its application by different leaders? Reconvene the whole group and share some of the ideas that students articulated. Then have students read Earhart's poem "Courage," and discuss what they think it means. Ask them how the poem adds to their understanding of the personal side of Ms. Earhart. (The poem can be found on the Internet.)

◎ If you have a particularly precocious student in the class who has a passion for poetry, direct him or her to "What Archives Reveal: The Hidden Poems of Amelia Earhart" by S. Morris (http://docs.lib.purdue.edu/lib_research/28), and have the student write a paragraph on whether or not the article impacted his or her understanding and/or appreciation of Ms. Earhart.

◎ Amelia Earhart said, "Women must pay for everything. They do get more glory than men for comparable feats. But they also get more notoriety when they crash." In small, same-gender groups, have students discuss if this assertion is still true today. Are there differences between men and women as leaders? Are there differences in their abilities to initiate actions and/or take risks? Have groups come to a consensus on their position, defend their position with examples, and report their conclusions to the whole class.

◎ For independent work, encourage students to read *Amelia Lost: The Life and Disappearance of Amelia Earhart* by Candace Fleming. Instead of writing a traditional book report, ask students to take a position on Ms. Earhart's decision to fly around the world and to discuss the generalization on risk taking as it relates to both her decision and their agreement or disagreement with it.

◎ Ask students to interview three adults about risk taking. Sample questions might include: What is the greatest risk you have taken so far in your life? What was the outcome or impact, if any, of taking that risk? Did you go through a conscious process of assessing the risk before you took it? If yes, how would you describe that process? Have students write up the results from the interviews and draw conclusions regarding the data they collected.

Taking Calculated Risks

Individual Situation

Should I, Amelia Earhart, try to be the first woman to fly around the world?

	Outcome (Gain or Loss)	Likelihood	Choice	Risk Management Option
Best Case	Successful flight will set a new world record, promote women's rights, bring her more fame and wealth	High if adequate precautions are in place	Go	Reduction (optimize success by careful planning, use of state-of-the-art equipment, backup systems in place for rescue at sea)
			Don't Go	Avoidance
Worst Case	Plane crash could lead to the death of herself and her crew	Low to moderate if adequate precautions are in place	Go	Retention (accept the risk and proceed in spite of it)
			Don't Go	Avoidance

Name: _____ Date: _____

Biographical Chart: Amelia Earhart

Full Name: _____

Lifespan: _____

Early Family Background and Created Family Structure

_____

_____

_____

Personality Characteristics and Areas of Aptitude, Talent, and Interest

_____

_____

_____

Major Career/Professional Events and Accomplishments

_____

_____

_____

Personal Life Themes/Beliefs

_____

_____

_____

Selected Quotations

_____

_____

_____

Awards and Recognition

_____

_____

_____

_____

Handout 4.2
Taking Calculated Risks

Conditions for Risk Assessment

Risk requires three conditions:

◎ the potential for loss or gain (may involve opportunities, reputation, or even life),

◎ the likelihood of the occurrence, and

◎ the ability to make a choice that impacts the occurrence of the potential loss or gain.

Options for Risk Management

Risk can be treated in four ways:

◎ avoidance (eliminate the risk, withdraw from the risk, or do not enter into the situation that presents the risk),

◎ reduction (optimize the potential for a positive outcome or weaken the potential for a negative outcome),

◎ sharing (transfer the risk elsewhere, redistribute the costs of the risk among parties, or purchase insurance against the risk), and

◎ retention (accept the risk and plan for the costs associated with its occurrence).

Individual Situation

Should I, Amelia Earhart, try to be the first woman to fly around the world?

	Outcome (Gain or Loss)	Likelihood	Choice	Risk Management Option
Best Case				
Worst Case				

Group Situation

	Outcome (Gain or Loss)	Likelihood	Choice	Risk Management Option
Best Case				
Worst Case				

Lesson 5
Bill Gates and Motivation

> *As we look ahead into the next century, leaders will be those who empower others.*
>
> —Bill Gates

Instructional Purpose

- ◎ To practice using the Internet to do biographical research
- ◎ To map biographical data against key leadership factors
- ◎ To understand the skill of motivation to move others toward a goal

Materials Needed

- ◎ Handout 5.1: Biographical Chart: Bill Gates
- ◎ Handout 5.2: Don't Give Up Now
- ◎ Teachers' Rap Sheet on Bill Gates (see Appendix A)

Activities and Instructional Strategies

Part 1 (2 periods)

1. The teacher will check to see that students have completed their Biographical Chart for Bill Gates.
2. The teacher will then have the whole class complete a master Biographical Chart on Mr. Gates using a white board or overhead projector to compile the information gathered by students. Ask: What did you discover about Mr. Gates's early family background and created family structure? What did you discover about his education? Follow this format until the chart has been completed. The teacher may choose to annotate or extend the information in the Biographical Chart by drawing on the data provided in the Teachers' Rap Sheet found in Appendix A.
3. The teacher should conclude this part of the lesson by pointing out that Ben Carson and Bill Gates are still alive, but that Walt Disney and Amelia Earhart passed away before the students were born so there is no overlap in their life spans. Ask the students if this makes it harder or easier to relate to the biographies of these leaders. Have them give a rationale for their responses.

Part II (1 period)

1. The teacher will engage students in a large-group discussion using the following questions as prompts:
   o In what ways is Bill Gates a leader?
   o To what extent did time, place, and circumstances impact his ability to become a leader?
   o How would you describe the vision that Bill Gates had for the computer/software industry?
   o What personal characteristics contributed to Bill Gates's ability to found Microsoft?
   o What evidence is there of both initiative and risk taking in Bill Gates's profile?
   o What evidence is there of Mr. Gates's ability to communicate effectively as a speaker, a writer, and a listener?
   o What do you see as Bill Gates's lasting impact and contributions in the areas of technology and philanthropy based on what you know at this time?
   o Bill Gates said,

   > We all learn best in our own ways. Some people do better studying one subject at a time, while some do better studying three things at once. Some people do best studying in structured, linear way, while others do best jumping around, "surrounding" a subject rather than traversing it. Some people prefer to learn by manipulating models, and others by reading.

   > How does this belief apply to you as a learner? Do you have a preferred way of learning new things?

Part III (2 periods)

This section of the lesson provides a practice exercise that teaches students about motivation and allows them to practice persuasive writing techniques.

1. The teacher should put the definitions of motivation, intrinsic motivation, and extrinsic motivation on the board:
   o *Motivation*: The process that begins, guides, and maintains goal-directed behavior.
   o *Intrinsic motivation*: Motivation that is driven by an interest in or enjoyment of the task itself and comes from within the individual.

    o *Extrinsic motivation*: Motivation that comes from the performance of an activity to obtain an outcome, such as a grade or a reward. It comes from outside the individual.

2. Discuss the definitions with students and note that leaders usually have self-motivation. This is the drive to take on a challenge and pursue it until one finds mastery or success. But to accomplish big goals, leaders must develop skills in motivating others (team motivation). A leader should be able to support or encourage intrinsic and extrinsic motivation in other individuals who make up the team.

3. There are many ways a leader can motivate and influence others. Sometimes a leader leads by example rather than words. Sometimes leaders develop a personal, ongoing relationship with a team member or colleague in order to mentor him or her. Frequently, the motivation comes from verbal or written communication. What is said and how it is said can have a powerful impact on getting others to engage in achieving the vision that is proposed.

4. Tell students that they are going to practice motivational skills today. Students may work alone, in dyads, or in triads to do the exercise and allow them to regroup based on their preferred approach. Distribute Handout 5.2: Don't Give Up Now, and go over the instructions with them. Give students 20–30 minutes to construct their written responses.

5. Reconvene the whole class. Ask one member of each group to read its written responses to the class. After all responses have been shared, debrief the exercise by asking the following questions of the whole class:
   o Did any of the e-mails contain an example of the use of intrinsic motivation? What was the best example used?
   o Did any of the e-mails contain an example of the use of extrinsic motivation? What was the best example used?
   o Did the e-mails use different strategies to get their points across? If so, how would you describe some of these strategies? (The next lesson will identify strategies, so if students are unable to come up with ideas at this point, don't be concerned.)
   o Which e-mail was the most convincing and why?
   o Which e-mail was the most entertaining and why?

6. Have students hand in their written products so that copies can be made for each person who participated in a dyad or triad for inclusion in the student portfolios. Mark on the written product whether it was drafted individually or by a cluster of students.

Part IV (1 period)

1. The teacher will allow 10–15 minutes for students to complete their journals using some or all of the following questions as prompts:
   o What did you learn from the biographical study of Bill Gates that is useful or interesting in your understanding of leadership?
   o What did you learn about Bill Gates that surprised you or helped you understand yourself better?
   o Is Bill Gates a role model for you? Why or why not?
   o What did you learn about motivation from this lesson? Is it easy or hard to motivate other people? Why?

2. Ask students to share their responses and discuss the questions as a whole class.

Assessment

The teacher should check to see that each student has completed the Biographical Chart (unless assigned as a group project) and the journal entry. In addition, each student or group of students should have prepared a written response for Part III of the lesson, which should be inserted into the student's portfolio.

Homework

Students should be informed that in the next lesson they will continue focusing on Bill Gates and motivational techniques. The next leader they will be studying is Clara Barton. They should get started now on their research for Ms. Barton by reading the following websites and completing Handout 7.1: Biographical Chart: Clara Barton. Also tell students the specific date by which this homework needs to be completed.
   ◎ Wikipedia (http://en.wikipedia.org/wiki/Clara_Barton)
   ◎ Life Stories of Civil War Heroes (http://dragoon1st.tripod.com/cw/index.html)
   ◎ Clara Barton Birthplace Museum (http://clarabartonbirthplace.org/site)
   ◎ The Barton Center for Diabetes Education (http://bartoncenter.org/bcsite/front_page)

Extensions

The following ideas are offered as substitutions for parts of the above lesson or as extensions for this lesson focusing on Bill Gates and the role of motivation in leadership.

◎ After ensuring that students understand the concept of foreign aid, have them go to YouTube and watch the video clip on "Why Is Foreign Aid Important?" (2 minutes). Ask students to take a position on whether or not they agree with Mr. Gates's opinion and have them write a persuasive essay defending their point of view.

◎ In dyads or small groups, have students reflect on a time in their lives when someone helped motivate them to finish a task, accomplish a project, or reach an important goal they had set for themselves. What did this person say or do that inspired them to stay the course? Conversely, was there a time when they gave up on something because they did not get the support and encouragement they needed? Reconvene the large group and ask for volunteers to share their stories. Summarize any common ideas or themes on motivation that evolve from this discourse.

◎ For independent work, encourage students to read a biography on Bill Gates targeted to young people. Two such biographies are identified in Appendix B of the unit. Instead of having students write a traditional book report, ask them to identify examples of how Bill Gates exhibited four or five of the individual generalizations on leadership addressed in this unit (e.g., vision, motivation, communication, action and risk taking, motivating others, perseverance and adversity, legacy) using examples that vary from those discussed in class.

Handout 5.1

Biographical Chart: Bill Gates

Full Name: _____

Lifespan: _____

Early Family Background and Created Family Structure

_____

_____

_____

Personality Characteristics and Areas of Aptitude, Talent, and Interest

_____

_____

_____

Major Career/Professional Events and Accomplishments

_____

_____

_____

Personal Life Themes/Beliefs

_____

_____

_____

Selected Quotations

_____

_____

_____

Awards and Recognition

_____

_____

_____

_____

Handout 5.2

Don't Give Up Now

Imagine that you are all grown up. Pick one of the following people as your best friend and read the e-mail message he or she has just sent you on your cell phone.

◎ **The mountain climber:** I am near the top of Mt. Everest. I am cold and tired. The wind is sharp, and the air is thin. My toes are frostbitten; the glare of the sun is blinding. My Sherpa says he will come no further than this point with me. I only have another 500 feet to reach the summit, but I don't think I can make it. Help me!

◎ **The novelist:** I feel like I have been working on this book my entire life, but I can't find the right way to end the story. I am only a chapter away from finishing the novel, but I must have writer's block. I can't find the ideas or the right words to pull everything together. I wanted this to be my best work, but I am frustrated and stymied. Help me!

◎ **The scientist:** I have conducted more than 500 experiments in my quest to find a cure for cancer of the pancreas. Every time I get a result that moves me a step forward, I get a new result that moves me a step back. I feel like I am going around in circles. Edward Jenner found a vaccine for smallpox; Jonas Salk found a vaccine for polio. I am just a failure. What is the point of it all? Help me!

◎ **The composer:** I have spent many years studying musical composers, from Bach and Beethoven to Gershwin and Bernstein. I have even analyzed the musical innovations of The Beatles, Taylor Swift, and Jay-Z. I think I can make an important contribution to modern music with the new symphony I am working on. I have the first two movements completed, but I just can't find the notes and chords that will comprise the third movement and allow me to end the piece with a flourish. I guess I just don't have the talent and energy I need to see it through. Help me!

◎ **The soldier:** I don't think this war will ever end. It is 100 degrees every day in this pitiful country where my platoon has been sent. I have to carry 40 pounds of armor and equipment as I patrol the perimeter every 8 hours. I can't sleep because of the gunfire and mortars in the night; I have to watch every step I take to avoid the explosive devices that have been planted under the sand by the enemy. I am lonely and exhausted, and I wonder if it is all worth fighting for. Help me!

Now it is your turn to write back. What can you say that will motivate your best friend to keep going or hang in there? Each of these individuals is facing the biggest turning point of his or her life, and you are the person each has called upon to save the day. Make your message count, and choose your words wisely.

Lesson 6
Using Public Speaking to Persuade Others

Instructional Purpose

- ◎ To learn about a set of strategies that contribute to effective speaking
- ◎ To analyze the use of these strategies by Bill Gates to motivate his audience
- ◎ To construct and deliver a speech that applies the strategies examined

Materials Needed

- ◎ Teacher's Annotated Version of Six Communication Strategies to Promote Motivation
- ◎ Sample Responses to Handout 6.3: Analyzing the Speech: "Mosquitos, Malaria, and Education"
- ◎ Handout 6.1: Six Communication Strategies to Promote Motivation
- ◎ Handout 6.2: List of Vocabulary Words From "Mosquitos, Malaria, and Education"
- ◎ Handout 6.3: Analyzing the Speech: "Mosquitos, Malaria, and Education"

Activities and Instructional Strategies

Part I (1–2 periods)

In *The 108 Skills of Natural Born Leaders* by Warren Blank (2001) and *The Leader as Communicator* by Robert Mai and Alan Akerson (2003), the authors stressed the importance of communication as a foundational skill that needs to be cultivated for effective leadership. In two earlier lessons, students focused on understanding how to motivate others both by using well-chosen words and messages and by practicing empathic listening.

1. Introduce this lesson to the students by connecting it to the previous lesson. In this lesson, they will be listening to a speech by Bill Gates on TED (http://www.ted.com) and analyzing it according to selected criteria.
2. Have a student read the following quotation by Bill Gates (it should already be written on the blackboard): "I believe that if you show people the problems and you show them the solutions, they will be moved to act."
3. Distribute Handout 6.1: Six Communication Strategies to Promote Motivation and discuss the ideas with the students. (An annotated ver-

sion of the handout can be found at the end of this lesson to help the teacher explain the six strategies and their application to public speaking.)

4. Ask a student to read the first strategy on the list. Before you have explained the strategy to the group, ask the students to explain it or give an example of it. As their responses develop, help to shape the discussion with the information that has been provided on the annotated version designed to help you. Repeat this process until all six of the strategies on the list have been explicated. As an alternative to this approach, you may prepare a mini-lecture on the strategies, but a constructivist approach, rather than a didactic approach, is recommended.

5. Conclude this part of the lesson by asking students if they can think of any other strategies that might contribute to public speaking in a way that helps to motivate the listener or audience the speaker is trying to influence. Do not add any additional strategies unless the students themselves propose them.

Part II (1 period)

1. The teacher will prepare the students to view the video clip of Bill Gates's speech entitled "Mosquitos, Malaria, and Education" (http://www.ted.com/talks/bill_gates_unplugged.html) by doing four things:

   o Explain to students that the audience for this speech is college students, so there will be some big ideas presented in the speech, and there will be some words they may not be familiar with. Assure them that they do not need to know every word in order to pick out the main theme of the speech.

   o Distribute Handout 6.2: List of Vocabulary Words From "Mosquitos, Malaria, and Education," which contains words embedded in the speech that may be unfamiliar to the students, and quickly go over this list with them. Tell them that they do not need to remember these words. You are giving them the words just to make it easier for them to listen to the speech. Reemphasize that they will be focusing on the big ideas in the speech. If you believe your students are already familiar with most of these words, omit this step.

   o Distribute copies of Handout 6.3: Analyzing the Speech: "Mosquitos, Malaria, and Education," and go over the questions with the students. This will help them attend to what they are expected to focus on and glean from the speech.

   o Tell students that the speech is approximately 20 minutes long, focuses on Mr. Gates's philanthropic work (not computer software), and requires their undivided attention.

2. Show the video clip of the speech.

3. At the conclusion of the speech, give students 20 minutes to answer individually the questions on the handout. Based on their progress, allow additional time as needed. If there is a break between the implementation of Parts II and III, students may be assigned the completion of the handout as interim homework. (Answers to the questions are included for the teacher at the end of the lesson. These answers are intended to help the teacher guide the large-group discussion of the student responses, not to grade their answers. The answer key should *not* be distributed to students.)

Part III (1 period)

1. Break the students into triads to discuss their answers to the questions. Ask each group to prepare a group response to the questions on the handout. You will want to distribute some blank copies of the handout to the groups. Allow no more than 20 minutes for this component of the lesson.

2. Reconvene the large group. Ask for a volunteer to share his or her group's answer to the first question on the handout. Ask if every group came up the same response. Clarify discrepancies to move students to a clearer understanding of the answer. Repeat this process by calling on different groups as you move through the rest of the questions on the handout used to critique Gates's speech.

3. When you get to Question 4 on the handout (focusing on the strategies he used), ask students the following additional question before moving to Question 5: Are there other strategies that you observed that were not on the list of strategies we have examined? Prompt them to think about Gates's quotation (in Part I of the lesson) and his use of flattery to "sweeten up" his audience.

4. End this part of the lesson by asking students to rate the speech on a scale of 1 to 10 with 1 being a very unsuccessful speech and 10 being a very motivating speech. Ask how many students gave it a 10, how many gave it a 9, and so forth.

5. Praise students for their hard work, as this is a very challenging lesson for upper elementary students, even high-ability ones.

Part IV (1–2 periods)

1. Tell students that now it is their turn to write and deliver a 2–3-minute speech about something that they are passionate about. The topic of their choice might be a personal interest (e.g., national parks, musical theater), a hobby (e.g., stamps, model airplanes), a cause (e.g., animal rights, clean

water), or a concern (e.g., childhood obesity, homeland security). Their goal is to try to get other members of the class to at least appreciate, if not share in, their enthusiasm. They should try to incorporate at least two of the strategies that they have learned but can use as many as they want. Give them 15–20 minutes to prepare their talks.

2. After the time has elapsed, have each student give the speech he or she has prepared. After each speech, ask the rest of the class which strategies they saw being used by the speaker.

3. Debrief the exercise by asking these questions of the whole class:
   o What were the most common strategies used by members of the class?
   o Whose speech created the most enthusiasm among listeners? Why?
   o Was anyone surprised by any of the topics chosen by class members for their speeches?
   o Did any of the speeches result in a newfound appreciation of or interest in the topic covered?
   o What did you learn about the process of motivating others through public speaking by trying to do it yourself?

Assessment

The teacher should check to see that each student has completed Handout 6.3: Analyzing the Speech: "Mosquitos, Malaria, and Education" and then insert it into the student's portfolio. The student's written speeches (or speech notes) should also be inserted into their portfolios.

Homework

Remind students that the Biographical Chart on Clara Barton is due for the next class period (Lesson 7). The additional homework for Lesson 6 is the completion of journal entries based on one or more of the following questions as prompts. These questions may be put on the board or can be made into a handout that is inserted into the students' journals.

◎ What new insights do you have about Bill Gates's leadership abilities after viewing his speech?

◎ Which two strategies to promote motivation would you find most appealing if you were in an audience? Why?

◎ Think back to what you wrote in the exercise on Handout 5.2: Don't Give Up Now. Has today's lesson given you some additional ideas about what you could have written to your friend? If yes, give one example of what you might include if you had to do it over.

◎ How did the assignment to write and deliver your own speech impact your understanding of the importance of and the skills needed for motivating others through public speaking?

Extensions

The following ideas are offered as extensions or substitutions for this lesson.

◎ Have students self-select another speech that was given by someone in a leadership position. Have the students adapt the questions on Handout 6.3 (they can eliminate Question 2, for instance) to the new speech and write answers to them. An example might be the speech by Dr. Martin Luther King, Jr. entitled "I Have a Dream," which is easily found on the Internet.

◎ Have students rewrite their responses to Handout 5.2: Don't Give Up Now, incorporating at least three of the new strategies that they have studied.

◎ Have each student identify a "big problem" that he or she might be interested in working on in his or her chosen career. A big problem requires expertise that cuts across lots of different fields such as the eradication of world hunger, the achievement of world peace, the increased participation of citizens in a democracy, the finding of a cure for a major disease and getting the cure distributed, and improving economic conditions for the poor. Group students together based on their choice of a problem. Ask them to discuss what kinds of expertise and talents are needed to address their problem and what skills they personally would like to develop to bring to the table.

◎ Have students rewrite the 2–3-minute speech they gave in class after they have heard all of the other speeches given by their classmates. Give them at least 24 hours to come up with a more effective construction. Allow them to present their new and improved version in front of the class after a future lesson has been completed. Discuss the revisions made with the whole class.

Teacher's Annotated Version
of Six Communication Strategies to Promote Motivation

(Not for distribution to students)

1. **Build trust in your audience or team.** Edward R. Murrow said, "To be persuasive, we must be believable; to be believable, we must be credible; to be credible, we must be truthful." Ways in which a leader can build trust through communication include being up front and truthful, speaking knowledgeably about the topic or issue, sharing his or her own expertise or credentials in an area to demonstrate competence, and treating questions, concerns, or feedback from others with respect and dignity.

2. **Show confidence, conviction, and enthusiasm**. Make your case or present your perspective with self-assurance and ease. Know what you want to say and avoid relying on prepared notes or a teleprompter too much. Imbue your words with energy and passion. Use nonverbal behavior that reinforces your words. Make eye contact with your audience. Don't be threatened by questions or challenges.

3. **Stay on message, and be clear and precise**. Organize your thoughts to build your case in a logical, straightforward way. Choose words that your audience will understand. Introduce your main point early, remind people of it as you develop your argument, and come back to it at the end. Don't ramble or falter. Don't say, "Uh, uh . . ."

4. **Use graphic aids, such as pictures, charts, and graphs, to illustrate and clarify important points.** Sometimes it helps to present a picture that illustrates the point you want to make or to quantify your information in a chart, graph, or table. Graphic aids can make an idea more concrete and less abstract. Also, many people are visual learners, so if they can see pictures or representations of the information, it helps them to understand and retain it better.

5. **Use stories, metaphors, and symbols to entertain and inspire.** The right story or example can be worth a thousand dry facts. Sometimes a story or parable is a better way to explain what you mean. Stories and symbols are more interesting to many people as they often trigger an emotional response. Think of Aesop's fable, *The Tortoise and the Hare*, or of the children's book, *The Little Engine That Could*. These are stories that encourage people to keep going when they want to quit. Telling the story may be more powerful than just saying "Don't give up." Symbols also have feelings attached to them. Think of "Old Glory" in the Star-Spangled Banner,

waving in the red glare of the rockets at night: That symbolism reminds us our flag was still there. An example drawn from your own experience can be made into a brief storyline to make your point more persuasively.

6. **Use humor in an appropriate way.** Making people laugh is a good way to make them comfortable. They are more willing to hear what you have to say if they are in a good mood. Humor can be like an exclamation point; it emphasizes and draws attention to what is being said, acting as an aid to memory. Humor can also be offensive, so it is important to use light-heartedness in a way that promotes fellowship and does not alienate your audience or team.

Analyzing the Speech: "Mosquitos, Malaria, and Education"

(Not for distribution to students)

1. This speech is about trying to solve two big problems. What are these two problems?

   The two problems addressed in the speech are reducing infant deaths by preventing the spread of malaria and helping all students have access to a good education.

2. What is the connection between these two problems that the speaker makes? In other words, why does he cover both problems in his speech?

   Smart people are needed to solve big problems, and a good education helps to make people smarter.

3. *Why* is the speaker telling his audience about these two problems? In other words, what does he want to get them to do?

   Gates wants to motivate the audience members to use their minds to help solve big problems in the world that require the expertise of lots of different skill areas.

4. What strategies or techniques does the speaker use to motivate the audience to get involved in solving "big problems" like the ones he is describing? (Give at least four strategies.)

   Gates appears truthful and competent, which builds trust; he uses humor (releasing mosquitos) to make the audience laugh and feel good; he uses charts and pictures to illustrate his ideas so that the audience feels informed and knowledgeable; he delivers the speech without notes or a teleprompter and with great ease, which gives assurance to the audience that he is confident and passionate about his message; he tells about the KIPP program as an example of a success story; and he stays on message by introducing the theme at the beginning and reminding the audience of it again at the end. In addition to the six strategies on Handout 6.1, he follows his own advice and describes doable solutions so that the audience will know these problems are solvable, he flatters his audience by telling them they are brilliant (praise), and he invites people with all kinds of skill sets to participate in achieving the solutions (inclusiveness). This combination of techniques to appeal to both emotion and reason makes the audience more likely to respond positively to the challenge he presents.

5. Did the speaker make you want to help solve big problems in the world?
   Answers will vary.

6. Based on this speech, what is the speaker's vision about the role of the United States?
   Gates believes that the United States can play an important role in solving world problems by doing a better job of educating all Americans.

Changing Tomorrow 1, Grades 4–5 © Prufrock Press Inc.

75

Permission is granted to photocopy or reproduce this page for single classroom use only.

Handout 6.1

Six Communication Strategies
to Promote Motivation

1. Build trust in your audience or team.

2. Show confidence, conviction, and enthusiasm.

3. Stay on message, and be clear and precise.

4. Use graphic aids, such as pictures, charts, and graphs, to illustrate and clarify important points.

5. Use stories, metaphors, and symbols to entertain and inspire.

6. Use humor in an appropriate way.

Name: _____ Date: _____

List of Vocabulary Words From "Mosquitos, Malaria, and Education"

◎ **Mortality:** Death

◎ **Temperate zones:** Areas of the Earth's surface where the temperatures are not extremely hot or extremely cold

◎ **Quartile:** One fourth of a group

◎ **Annotate:** To explain or comment on

◎ **Seniority:** Having privilege or priority as a result of time spent in a position

◎ **Tenure:** An employee's right to keep a job based on years in that job

Name: _____ Date: _____

Analyzing the Speech: "Mosquitos, Malaria, and Education"

1. This speech is about trying to solve two big problems. What are these two problems?

   _____

   _____

   _____

2. What is the connection between these two problems that the speaker makes? In other words, why does he cover both problems in his speech?

   _____

   _____

   _____

3. *Why* is the speaker telling his audience about these two problems? In other words, what does he want to get them to do?

   _____

   _____

   _____

   _____

4. What strategies or techniques does the speaker use to motivate the audience to get involved in solving "big problems" like the ones he is describing? (Give at least four strategies.)

   _____

   _____

   _____

   _____

   _____

   _____

   _____

   _____

Changing Tomorrow 1, Grades 4–5 © Prufrock Press Inc.

5. Did the speaker make you want to help solve big problems in the world?

_____

6. Based on this speech, what is the speaker's vision about the role of the United States?

_____

_____

_____

_____

_____

Lesson 7
Clara Barton and Action

I have an almost complete disregard of precedent, and a faith in the possibility of something better. It irritates me to be told how things have always been done. I defy the tyranny of precedent. I go for anything new that might improve the past.

—Clara Barton

Instructional Purpose

- ◎ To practice using the Internet to do biographical research
- ◎ To map the biographical data against key leadership factors
- ◎ To understand Clara Barton's leadership role as an initiator of the American Red Cross

Materials Needed

- ◎ Handout 7.1: Biographical Chart: Clara Barton
- ◎ Handout 7.2: Applying Generalizations About Leadership
- ◎ Teachers' Rap Sheet on Clara Barton (see Appendix A)

Activities and Instructional Strategies

Part I (1–2 class periods)

1. The teacher will have the whole class complete a master Biographical Chart on Clara Barton, based on the information students found from completing their prior homework assignment research. This should be done using a white board or overhead projector. The teacher should use questioning techniques to gather the data needed to complete a master chart. The teacher may choose to annotate the information collected by drawing on the Teachers' Rap Sheet for Clara Barton if students have failed to grasp and/or record important pieces of biographical information.

2. Conclude this lesson by asking students to comment on the most critical events in her life and explain why they identified them as being the most critical.

Part II (1 period)

1. The teacher will engage students in a large-group discussion using the following questions:
   - o In what ways was Clara Barton a leader?

o If you were to cite her major strengths as a leader, what would they be? What is your evidence?

o What qualities made her able to accomplish so much at a time when few women were given authority in society?

o What were the experiences she had in her early life that contributed to her leadership capacity?

o Because she had assumed many roles in her life (teacher, patent officer, nurse), she had a unique vantage point from which to think about the founding of the American Red Cross. What would have been her reasons to do it, based on those experiences?

o How does Clara Barton embody the capacity to have vision and take risks to achieve it?

o Clara Barton said, "An institution or reform movement that is not selfish, must originate in the recognition of some evil that is adding to the sum of human suffering, or diminishing the sum of happiness." What do you think she meant by this?

o What were the most powerful influences on Clara Barton in her development as a leader? Cite evidence to support your perspective.

Part III (1 period)

1. Ask students to use Handout 7.2: Applying Generalizations About Leadership to discuss how the unit generalizations relate to the life of Clara Barton. Have the students work in dyads for 15 minutes.

2. Ask students to select one of the following quotes by Clara Barton and write a paragraph describing what she meant and how it relates to the generalizations about leadership. Give students 20 minutes to compose their response.

o "The door that nobody else will go in at, seems always to swing open widely for me."

o "The surest test of discipline is its absence."

o "I have an almost complete disregard of precedent, and a faith in the possibility of something better. It irritates me to be told how things have always been done. I defy the tyranny of precedent. I go for anything new that might improve the past."

3. Ask 5–6 students to read their responses aloud to the class. Discuss each quote with respect to its meaning and significance in illuminating Clara Barton's life. How does the quote demonstrate one of the generalizations about leadership?

4. Ask students to put their writing in their portfolios.

Part IV (1 period)

1. Ask students to write to the following prompt in their journal: To what extent did Clara Barton use adversity in her personal life to make a contribution to society? Reflect on your understanding of the major events in her life to respond. Give students 15 minutes to write.
2. Discuss the prompt with the whole class. What is the role of adversity in motivating people to perform tasks beyond their seeming capabilities? What other figures in history might fit this profile as well?

Assessment

The teacher should check to see that each student has completed the Biographical Chart on Clara Barton and include it in the student's portfolio. The teacher should verify that Handout 7.2: Applying Generalizations About Leadership and the journal entries have been completed to ensure student understanding of the abstract ideas.

Homework

Students are assigned responsibility for completing Handout 8.1: Biographical Chart: Tecumseh in preparation for the next class period. The three sites that students should be directed to for conducting this research are as follows:

- Wikipedia (http://en.wikipedia.org/wiki/Tecumseh)
- History.com (http://www.history.com/topics/tecumseh)
- About.com (http://history1800s.about.com/od/leaders/p/tecumsehbio.htm)

Extensions

The following ideas are offered as substitutions for parts of the above lesson or as extensions for this lesson focusing on Clara Barton and the role of adversity in leadership.

- Ask students to read a biography on Clara Barton. Have them to develop an argument for her inclusion in the Hall of Fame for Great Americans.
- Have students choose one of the other generalizations about leadership (one they did not write about in Part III of the lesson) and argue that Clara Barton exemplified it in some way.
- Have students consider the life of one of the following suffragettes who lived at the same time as Clara Barton: Susan B. Anthony, Elizabeth Cady Stanton, or Ida B. Wells. What were the patterns of development, education, critical events, and characteristics they possessed? How were they similar to and different from Clara Barton? How were their activi-

ties similar and different from those of Clara Barton? Which efforts do they think were most important in retrospect to elevate the dignity of women and their capacity in society today? Students should prepare a poster to illustrate their points.

Name: _____ Date: _____

Biographical Chart: Clara Barton

Full Name: _____

Lifespan: _____

Early Family Background and Created Family Structure

_____

_____

_____

Personality Characteristics and Areas of Aptitude, Talent, and Interest

_____

_____

_____

Major Career/Professional Events and Accomplishments

_____

_____

_____

Personal Life Themes/Beliefs

_____

_____

_____

Selected Quotations

_____

_____

_____

Awards and Recognition

_____

_____

_____

_____

Name: _____ Date: _____

Applying Generalizations About Leadership

Generalizations	Applications to the Life of Clara Barton
1. Leadership requires vision—the ability to see beyond what is to what might be by bridging the present and the future.	
2. Leadership requires the ability to communicate effectively with multiple individuals and groups regarding new ideas and plans for implementation.	
3. Leadership is based in action and often requires risk taking.	
4. Leadership requires the ability to influence and motivate others through words and actions.	
5. Leadership requires perseverance in the face of challenges and hardships.	

Changing Tomorrow 1, Grades 4–5 © Prufrock Press Inc.

Lesson 8
Tecumseh and Legacy

Sell a country! Why not sell the air, the great sea, as well as the earth? Didn't the Great Spirit make them all for the use of his children?

—Tecumseh

Instructional Purpose

- ◎ To practice using the Internet to do biographical research
- ◎ To map the biographical data against key leadership factors
- ◎ To understand the leadership of Tecumseh as a Shawnee Indian, fighting for tribal unity against the Americans in the War of 1812
- ◎ To examine the idea of legacy in leadership and how it is shaped by the passage of time

Materials Needed

- ◎ Handout 8.1: Biographical Chart: Tecumseh
- ◎ Handout 8.2: Outline Structure for Speech
- ◎ Teacher's Rap Sheet on Tecumseh (see Appendix A)

Activities and Instructional Strategies

Part I (1–2 periods)

1. The teacher will have the whole class complete a master Biographical Chart on Tecumseh, based on the information students found from completing their prior homework assignment research. This should be done using a white board or overhead projector. The teacher should use questioning techniques to gather the data needed to complete a master chart. The teacher may choose to annotate the information collected by drawing on the Teacher's Rap Sheet for Tecumseh if students have failed to grasp and/or record important pieces of biographical information.

2. Ask students what they thought was most impressive about his life. Comment on their reasoning.

3. The teacher should share the following with the students: Tecumseh is the first warrior as leader that we have studied. How does that make him different? Does the presence of the situation of war create leaders, or are they already formed to be leaders? What do you think? Ask students to discuss these questions in their groups and arrive at a consensus.

4. Ask a spokesperson from each group to present a 3-minute argument supporting the group's perspective.
5. Discuss the range of views on the issue and record them on a number line.

Part II (1 period)

1. The teacher will engage students in a large-group discussion using the following questions:
   o How did the oral tradition of Native Americans and of the time period favor Tecumseh?
   o Tecumseh died at age 45, which is young by today's standards but typical for that time period. What do you think he would have wanted his legacy to be?
   o Did Tecumseh make a difference or die in vain? Why?
   o What does the word *martyr* mean? Do you think Tecumseh was a martyr? Why or why not?
   o How does Tecumseh's life illustrate our generalizations about leadership? Which one is most appropriate for him and why?

2. Based on their study of Tecumseh, ask students to write an epitaph for him and illustrate it with an image they think is appropriate. Students should describe their image and explain why they chose it. Have a few students share their epitaphs and images. Post them around the room for all to view.

Part III (1 period)

1. Access "Death of Tecumseh," a section of the frieze in the rotunda of the United States Capitol (see http://www.aoc.gov/cc/art/rotunda/frieze/Death-of-Tecumseh.cfm). Project it on a large screen or print copies for students to view. Provide students with background information.
2. Ask students to study the frieze. After carefully observing the figures' clothing, body language, facial expressions, and position in the frieze, have each student sketch relevant aspects of the frieze and write a journal entry of their interpretation of Tecumseh's death based on the artist's rendition.
3. Ask: Why is this artistic frieze commemorated on the United States Capitol building? Have students discuss their thoughts with a partner and share the responses with the whole class.
4. Ask: How does such commemoration contribute to legacy? Have students share their responses with the whole class.

Part IV (1 period)

1. Show students the following video and audio clips:
   o "Shawnee Chief Tecumseh Address to General William Henry Harrison" from American Rhetoric Online Speech Bank (http://www.americanrhetoric.com/speeches/nativeamericans/chieftecumseh.htm)
   o "Episode 2: Tecumseh's Vision" from *We Shall Remain*, a PBS documentary series (http://www.pbs.org/wgbh/amex/weshallremain/the_films/episode_2_trailer)

2. Ask: How do these multimedia sources illustrate Tecumseh's capacity to motivate and persuade others? What techniques did he employ? Have students share their responses with the whole class.

3. Give students 30 minutes to write a 3-minute speech to persuade others that war is bad. They should use Tecumseh's techniques to the extent possible. After they are finished, have them share their speeches in small groups. Use Handout 8.2: Outline Structure for Speech to guide the speech construction.

Assessment

The teacher should check to see that each student has completed the Biographical Chart on Tecumseh and include it in the student's portfolio. The teacher may use the written epitaph project and the speech to assess student understanding of Tecumseh and his leadership. Class discussion also may be used for this purpose.

Homework

Prior to the next class, a panel of local leaders should be convened by the teacher to discuss the generalizations about leadership around which the unit is framed and to discuss characteristics of leadership as they see it practiced in their fields. The local group should be 3–5 community leaders representing law, education, business, politics, the world of scientific research, or other fields from which you can find someone to participate. It is often helpful to contact a nearby university or civic agencies to find local leaders. The purpose of the panel is to provide students the opportunity to interview leaders and get their thoughts on the concept of what it means to be a leader today. Send a copy of the unit generalizations ahead of time to the panel members, asking them to be ready to comment on each of them in their view of leadership so they feel versed in the direction you want the discussion to go.

Students should put together five questions they have about leadership, based on the study of six very different leaders to ask the local panel for tomorrow's class.

Extensions

The following ideas are offered as substitutions for parts of the above lesson or as extensions for this lesson focusing on Tecumseh and the role of legacy in leadership.

- Students may choose to read a biography of Tecumseh and create a timeline of his life, noting in red the most significant events and explaining why they are so important.
- Students may read a novel based on the life of Tecumseh and describe how the author has fictionalized his life. Compare the novel version with the version they have researched. How are they similar and different? Two suggestions are included below:
  - Ann Rinaldi's novel, *The Second Bend in the River*, depicts a fictionalized version of a romance between Tecumseh and Rebecca Galloway.
  - Orson Scott Card's novel, *Red Prophet*, features Tecumseh (named Ta-Kumsaw)

- Students may want to know more about the historical period in which Tecumseh lived. Have them select a book on the period or conduct Internet research to learn more. Ask them to answer the following question in a short response paper: How did the time period influence Tecumseh and how did he influence the time period?

Handout 8.1

Biographical Chart: Tecumseh

Full Name: _____

Lifespan: _____

Early Family Background and Created Family Structure

_____

_____

_____

Personality Characteristics and Areas of Aptitude, Talent, and Interest

_____

_____

_____

Major Career/Professional Events and Accomplishments

_____

_____

_____

Personal Life Themes/Beliefs

_____

_____

_____

Selected Quotations

_____

_____

_____

Awards and Recognition

_____

_____

_____

_____

Handout 8.2

Outline Structure for Speech

Resolution: War is bad.

Introduction of the opinion:

_____

_____

_____

Reasons for the opinion:

_____

_____

_____

Examples:

_____

_____

_____

Elaboration of reasons:

_____

_____

_____

Connections:

_____

_____

_____

Conclusion:

_____

_____

_____

_____

Lesson 9
Local Panel of Leaders

....

Instructional Purpose

◎ To provide real-world contemporary examples of leadership
◎ To provide a comparative analysis of leadership past and present in specific fields

Materials Needed

◎ Handout 9.1: Interview Questions

Activities and Instructional Strategies

Part I (1 period)

1. Introduce the panel to the class and ask each panel member to comment on his or her leadership role and how each views the process. Provide the panel members the generalizations that the class has been studying about leadership and ask that they comment on a few of them with respect to their own area of leadership (they should have prepared this in advance).
2. Allow students to ask their questions that they composed for homework or the sample set provided to them in Handout 9.1: Interview Questions so that the panel can respond to student issues and concerns about leadership.
3. Provide a wrap-up to the panel discussion, emphasizing ideas discussed and areas of similarity and difference among the panelists' view of the leadership generalizations the class has been studying.
4. Thank the panel for coming, and be sure to have students write each panelist a thank-you note for his or her time.

Assessment

Have students add the questions they raised and the panelists' responses to their portfolio. Ask students to reflect on the experience by recording in their portfolios what they learned about contemporary leadership from the interviews.

Homework

Students should review the Biographical Charts of each leader studied in the unit.

Handout 9.1
Interview Questions

1. What is your leadership role?

2. How did you prepare for the role?

3. What are your major areas of responsibility? What do you do every day to be a leader in your field?

4. What skills of leadership do you possess?

5. How does your field determine who is a leader?

6. What do you think are the most important qualities of leadership and why?

7. What advice do you have for young people on becoming a leader?

8. Who do you most admire as a leader and why?

Lesson 10
Analysis and Synthesis of Leadership

Instructional Purpose

◎ To compare and contrast leadership skills and emphases across the six leaders studied

◎ To synthesize student understanding about the concept of leadership and the unit's generalizations

Materials Needed

◎ Handout 10.1: Need to Know Board of Essential Questions
◎ Handout 10.2: Comparative Analysis Chart of Leadership
◎ Handout 10.3: Leadership Self-Assessment Profile

Activities and Instructional Strategies

Part I (1 period)

1. Pass out copies of Handout 10.1: Need to Know Board of Essential Questions and ask students to work on it first individually, then discuss it with a partner, and then discuss it as a whole group. Students should begin to see the commonalities across leadership with respect to skills, actions, and beliefs. Ask: What are the critical skills, actions, and beliefs that strong leaders must hold? Why are they so necessary? Do all of our leaders possess these qualities? Can you comment on how that is so?

Part II (1 period)

1. Pass out copies of Handout 10.2: Comparative Analysis Chart of Leadership and ask students to work in groups of 3–5 to complete the chart. Ask: To what extent are there similarities and differences among the leaders studied with respect to key leadership ideas (generalizations)? To what extent are the differences based on the domain of leadership? Explain.

Part III (1 period)

1. Now that students have analyzed the qualities of great leaders and generalizations about the idea of leadership, they should write a journal entry

about the aspect of leadership that they feel is most important for them to develop and why. They may want to describe their career interests in light of this choice.

2. Have students share a few journal entries and discuss what it might take to be a leader in a few areas like science, the arts, and invention. Ask: Why are these areas of leadership valuable today? How do they match up with your aptitudes and interests, your values and beliefs, and your experiences so far in life?

Assessment

Students will add their work from today to their portfolios for teachers to review. They also will take the self-assessment found in Handout 10.3: Leadership Self-Assessment Profile. If there is time, the results of the assessment could be discussed and collected by the teacher for overall analysis with respect to leadership self-perceptions of the class. This tool may be included as a part of the unit assessment data.

Homework

Students should prepare for the postassessment by reviewing their overall understanding of the concept of leadership that they have studied in this unit. Students should ask themselves: How would I define leadership?

Name: _____ Date: _____

Need to Know Board of Essential Questions

....

Think about the leaders we have studied in this unit—Walt Disney, Ben Carson, Amelia Earhart, Bill Gates, Clara Barton, and Tecumseh. What do they have in common? Answer the question by reflecting on the following aspects of the leadership of each.

1. What do leaders do?

_____

_____

_____

_____

_____

_____

2. What skills do they possess?

_____

_____

_____

_____

_____

_____

3. What do leaders believe?

_____

_____

_____

_____

_____

_____

Name: _____ Date: _____

Comparative Analysis
Chart of Leadership

Complete the following chart in small groups, discussing what aspects of each Biographical Chart would allow you to see the leadership quality noted as strong in the particular person.

Leader	Visionary	Communicator	Risk Taker	Motivator
Disney				
Carson				
Earhart				
Gates				
Barton				
Tecumseh				

Name: _____ Date: _____

Leadership Self–Assessment Profile

On a scale of 1 to 4, with 1 being *poor*, 2 being *fair*, 3 being *good*, and 4 being *excellent*, how would you rate yourself on the following skills?

Category and Skill	Self-Rating
Visionary	
• I can usually grasp the big picture of a situation or problem.	
• I can usually propose new ideas or solutions.	
• I can see in my mind how changes that are made today will have an impact in the future.	
Communicator	
• I can write clearly and organize my ideas well.	
• I can speak clearly and organize my ideas well.	
• I can listen with my heart as well as my ears.	
• I can read and comprehend what I am reading quickly and thoroughly.	
Initiator and Risk Taker	
• I act to make improvements in things or fix problems before I am asked to do so by others.	
• I make an assessment of a risk before I act impulsively.	
• I put my energies into activities that are meaningful and of value.	
• I use judgment in making decisions about choices I have available to me.	
Motivator	
• I can persuade other people to follow my lead.	
• I can share the glory with all members of a team.	
• I can stay optimistic even when things are not going as planned.	
Perseverer	
• I am willing to put in the time and the energy to finish a task even though it may be complex and/or difficult.	
• I am willing to face and overcome obstacles that are put in my path.	
• I can see failure as an opportunity for growth and change.	

Pick one of the areas above that you feel can be strengthened in your own leadership profile and describe what you can do to improve your level of skill.

References

Bennis, W., & Goldsmith, J. (2003). *Learning to lead: A workbook on becoming a leader*. New York, NY: Basic Books.

Blank, W. (2001). *The 108 skills of natural born leaders*. New York, NY: Amacom.

Covey, S. R. (2004). *The 7 habits of highly effective people* (Rev. ed.). New York, NY: Simon and Schuster.

Mai, R., & Akerson, A. (2003). *The leader as communicator: Strategies and tactics to build loyalty, focus effort, and spark creativity*. New York, NY: Amacom.

National Association for Gifted Children. (2010). *NAGC Pre-K–Grade 12 Gifted Programming Standards: A blueprint for quality gifted education programs*. Washington, DC: Author.

National Governors Association Center for Best Practices, & Council of Chief State School Officers. (2010). *Common Core State Standards for English Language Arts*. Retrieved from http://www.corestandards.org/the-standards

Partnership for 21st Century Skills. (2011). *Overview*. Retrieved from http://www.p21.org/overview/skills-framework

Taba, H. (1962). *Curriculum development: Theory and practice*. New York, NY: Harcourt, Brace.

Part IV
Appendices

Appendix A
Teachers' Rap Sheets

Teachers' Rap Sheet
Walt Disney

Full Name: Walter Elias Disney

Life Span: December 5, 1901–December 15, 1966

Early Family Background and Created Family Structure

◎ Born in Chicago into a very poor family; his father was not successful at anything and abusive to kids
◎ Family originally came from Ireland to escape religious persecution
◎ Had three brothers and a sister
◎ 1925: Married Lillian Bounds, one of his employees, in Lewiston, ID
◎ Had two daughters: Diane Marie and Sharon Mae

Education

◎ Attended McKinley High School in Chicago and took night courses at the Art Institute of Chicago
◎ Dropped out of high school to join the Army but was rejected for being underage

Personality Characteristics and Areas of Aptitude, Talent, and Interest

◎ Showed an early interest in drawing and photography
◎ Was a cartoonist for high school paper
◎ Deeply remorseful when he carelessly killed a baby owl, which led to an interest in giving human traits to cartoon characters
◎ Had a withdrawn, suspicious, and controlling nature
◎ Possessed artistic talent and technical acumen
◎ Rarely showed emotion, although he did have a temper that would blow over quickly; at home, was affectionate and understanding
◎ Had an inquisitive mind and keen sense for education through entertainment
◎ Was dyslexic
◎ Had an instinctive awareness of popular taste
◎ Described as a chain-smoking "workaholic" who was prone to strong mood swings

Major Career/Professional Events and Accomplishments

◎ Joined the Red Cross after rejection from the Army and spent a year in France driving an ambulance

---

◎ 1923: Cofounded The Disney Brothers Studio (now known as The Walt Disney Company) with his brother, which is one of the best-known motion picture producers in the world, with an annual revenue of approximately $36 billion in the 2010 financial year

◎ 1928: Made the first Mickey Mouse animated full-length film, *Steamboat Willie*, doing the voice himself (added innovative music and sound effects)

◎ 1937: Premiered *Snow White and the Seven Dwarfs*, the first full-length animated musical feature, produced at an unheard cost of almost $1,490,000 during the Depression; Disney made animated films until 1955

◎ 1940–1942: Completed other full-length animated classics such as *Pinocchio*, *Fantasia*, *Dumbo*, and *Bambi*

◎ 1940s: Created inexpensive package films, containing collections of cartoon shorts, and issued them to theaters; ventured into full-length dramatic films that mixed live action and animated scenes

◎ Late 1940s: Resumed production on the full-length features *Alice In Wonderland* and *Peter Pan*, both of which had been shelved during the war years

◎ Studio achieved renewed popularity in 1949 with the creation of Donald Duck, the new star

◎ Mid-1950s: Produced a number of educational films on the space program in collaboration with NASA rocket designer Werner von Braun

◎ Hosted *The Wonderful World of Disney* (broadcast under several different names) for 10 years (early adopter of TV as a medium)

◎ 1955: Created Disneyland in Anaheim, CA, the first theme park

◎ 1960: Made Head of Pageantry for the 1960 Winter Olympics

◎ 1964: Premiered *Mary Poppins*, the most successful Disney film of the 1960s

◎ 1964: Debuted a number of exhibits at the World's Fair in New York that included audio-animatronic figures, which were later integrated into attractions at Disneyland and Disney World

◎ Conceived the idea for EPCOT Center, which opened almost 20 years after his death

Personal Life Themes/Beliefs

◎ After the incident with the owl, Disney vowed never to kill another living thing

◎ Insisted on being upbeat in his films; liked to feature small-town values and traditions, a concept he experienced very briefly while living in Marceline, MO, growing up

Selected Quotations

◎ "I am proud of the whole thing—the fact that I was able to build an organization and hold it."

◎ "A hundred years ago, Wagner conceived of a perfect and all-embracing art, combining music, drama, painting, and the dance, but in his wildest imagination he had no hint what infinite possibilities were to become commonplace through the invention of recording, radio, cinema and television. There already have been geniuses combining the arts in the mass-communications media, and they have already given us powerful new art forms. The future holds bright promise for those whose imaginations are trained to play on the vast orchestra of the art-in-combination. Such supermen will appear most certainly in those environments which provide contact with all the arts, but even those who devote themselves to a single phase of art will benefit from broadened horizons."

◎ "I don't believe there is a challenge anywhere in the world that is more important to people everywhere than finding the solutions to the problems of our cities. But where do we begin? Well, we're convinced we must start with the public need. And the need is not just for curing the old ills of old cities. We think the need is for starting from scratch on virgin land and building a community that will become a prototype for the future."

◎ "We are not trying to entertain the critics. I'll take my chances with the public."

◎ "You can design and create and build the most wonderful place in the world. But it takes people to make the dream a reality."

◎ "All cartoon characters and fables must be exaggeration, caricatures. It is the very nature of fantasy and fable."

◎ "When you're curious, you find lots of interesting things to do. And one thing it takes to accomplish something is courage."

◎ "I don't like formal gardens. I like wild nature. It's just the wilderness instinct in me, I guess."

◎ "We allow no geniuses around our Studio."

◎ "Movies can and do have tremendous influence in shaping young lives in the realm of entertainment towards the ideals and objectives of normal adulthood."

◎ "I never called my work an 'art.' It's part of show business, the business of building entertainment."

◎ "Whenever I go on a ride, I'm always thinking of what's wrong with the thing and how it can be improved."

◎ "The way to get started is to quit talking and begin doing."

◎ "Laughter is America's most important export."

◎ "People still think of me as a cartoonist, but the only thing I lift a pen or pencil for these days is to sign a contract, a check, or an autograph."

- "Why do we have to grow up? I know more adults who have the children's approach to life. They're people who don't give a hang what the Joneses do. You see them at Disneyland every time you go there. They are not afraid to be delighted with simple pleasures, and they have a degree of contentment with what life has brought—sometimes it isn't much, either."
- "The era we are living in today is a dream coming true."
- "There is more treasure in books than in all the pirates' loot on Treasure Island and at the bottom of the Spanish Main . . . and best of all, you can enjoy these riches every day of your life."
- "You're dead if you aim only for kids. Adults are only kids grown up, anyway."
- "Our heritage and ideals, our code and standards—the things we live by and teach our children—are preserved or diminished by how freely we exchange ideas and feelings."
- "I have been up against tough competition all my life. I wouldn't know how to get along without it."
- "Crowded classrooms and half-day sessions are a tragic waste of our greatest national resource—the minds of our children."
- "You reach a point where you don't work for money."
- "Of all of our inventions for mass communication, pictures still speak the most universally understood language."
- "I have no use for people who throw their weight around as celebrities, or for those who fawn over you just because you are famous."
- "Adults are interested if you don't play down to the little 2 or 3 year olds or talk down. I don't believe in talking down to children. I don't believe in talking down to any certain segment. I like to kind of just talk in a general way to the audience. Children are always reaching."
- "A man should never neglect his family for business."
- "I believe in being a motivator."

Awards and Recognition

- Won 26 personal Oscars over his lifetime
- Inaugural recipient of a star on the Anaheim Walk of Stars awarded in recognition of his significant contribution to the city of Anaheim
- 1935: Received the Légion d'honneur awarded by France
- 1935: Received a special medal from the League of Nations for the creation of Mickey Mouse
- 1964: Received the Presidential Medal of Freedom
- 1968: Received the Congressional Medal of Honor
- 2006: Inducted into the California Hall of Fame
- 1980: A star discovered by a Soviet astronomer is named after him

◎ 2003: Named in his honor, The Walt Disney Concert Hall in Los Angeles, CA, opened

◎ 2004: A biographical documentary, *Walt—The Man Behind the Myth*, was produced and is available on DVD

Lasting Impact and Contributions

◎ Name is still iconic in the field of family entertainment

◎ Established a company that generates huge revenues and employs thousands of people worldwide

◎ His innovations in the art of animation propelled the medium to new heights

◎ *Snow White and the Seven Dwarfs* is still considered one of the great feats and imperishable monuments of the motion picture industry

Changing Tomorrow 1, Grades 4–5 © Prufrock Press Inc.

Permission is granted to photocopy or reproduce this page for single classroom use only.

111

Teachers' Rap Sheet
Ben Carson

Full Name: Benjamin Solomon Carson, M.D.

Date of birth: September 18, 1951 to present

Early Family Background and Created Family Structure

- Born in Detroit, MI
- Mother was 13 when she married a 28-year-old man who worked in a car plant and was a nonordained minister (was also a bigamist)
- Has one younger brother, Curtis (who became an engineer)
- Father left home when Ben was 8 and did not pay child support
- Mother had been raised in foster care, so she worked two and three jobs at a time to keep her kids out of that system
- Family lived in tenements or lower class neighborhoods
- Mother was diligent and set high expectations for her kids
- Mother required boys to read two books a week and write book reports; she pretended to read them so they thought she was checking their work; TV was limited to three shows a week
- Ben experienced racism when a White teacher chided the White students for letting a Black student do better than them; was told by a gang of White boys to drop out of school
- 1975: Married Lacena (Candy) Rustin, a Yale classmate and accomplished musician
- Has three sons: Murray, Benjamin Jr., and Rhoeyce

Education

- Attended inner city schools
- Was at the bottom of his fifth-grade class and was called "dummy" by classmates
- Astonished teacher by identifying a rock sample, which became an awakening to himself and others that he was indeed intelligent; rose to the top of his class within a year
- Prevented from playing sports because of threats from White parents
- Joined ROTC in 10th grade (was one of only three kids in Detroit who achieved the rank of colonel in ROTC)
- Graduated with honors from Southwestern High School in inner-city Detroit
- Offered a full scholarship to West Point but did not take it

◎ 1973: Earned a bachelor's degree from Yale University in psychology, funded mostly through his academic scholarship

◎ 1977: Graduated from the University of Michigan Medical School with M.D. in neurology

Personality Characteristics and Areas of Aptitude, Talent, and Interest

◎ Overcame a troubled childhood in the inner city due to his perseverance and initiative

◎ Had a pathological temper as an adolescent (tried to stab another kid in the ninth grade)

◎ Used prayer to move beyond his anger and develop patience

◎ Read *Psychology Today* starting at age 13

◎ Dreamed of being a doctor from the age of 8

◎ Favorite childhood toy was a chemistry set

◎ Favorite childhood TV show was *G. E. College Bowl*

◎ Had superb hand-eye coordination and three-dimensional reasoning skills

◎ Ranked in the lower 90th percentile on the SAT

◎ Is a creative problem solver (could put information from different disciplines together to innovate in his field)

◎ Aficionado of classical music

◎ Has a strong work ethic

Major Career/Professional Events and Accomplishments

◎ 1977: Became a resident at The Johns Hopkins Hospital, Baltimore, MD

◎ 1982: Was a chief neurosurgeon at The Johns Hopkins Hospital

◎ 1983: Spent a year as a neurosurgeon in Perth, Australia

◎ 1984: Returned to The Johns Hopkins Hospital

◎ Age 33: Became the hospital's youngest division director when appointed as Director of Pediatric Neurology

◎ 1987: First surgeon in the world to successfully separate Siamese twins conjoined at the back of the head (the 70-member surgical team worked for 22 hours to perform this operation; Carson led the effort)

◎ Other surgical innovations have included the first intrauterine procedure to relieve pressure on the brain of a hydrocephalic fetal twin and the removal of one brain hemisphere from a seizure-laden young girl

◎ 1994: Established the Carson Scholars Fund to award scholarships to students in upper elementary school and beyond who demonstrated strong academics and community service; the fund also establishes reading rooms in school buildings to promote the joy of reading

◎ Created Angels of the OR to provide financial support for medical surgery for those who are indigent

◎ Has written four books: *Gifted Hands: The Ben Carson Story*; *Think Big: Unleashing Your Potential for Excellence*; *Take the Risk Learning to Identify, Choose, and Live With Acceptable Risk*; and *America the Beautiful: Rediscovering What Made This Nation Great* (2012)

Personal Life Themes/Beliefs

◎ Has a very strong belief in God and reads the Bible every day
◎ Member of Seventh Day Adventist Church
◎ Has stated that he doesn't believe in evolution
◎ Has a work-driven philosophy of life with a desire to be of service to others

Selected Quotations

◎ "My mother was the earliest, strongest, and most impacting force in my life."
◎ "There is no such person as a self-made individual."
◎ "It does not matter where we come from or what we look like. If we recognize our abilities, are willing to learn and to use what we know in helping others, we will always have a place in the world."
◎ "If we recognize our talents and use them appropriately, and choose a field that uses those talents, we will rise to the top of our field."
◎ "I'm a good neurosurgeon. That's not a boast but a way of acknowledging the innate ability God has given to me. Beginning with determination and using my gifted hands, I went on for training and for sharpening my skills."
◎ "Here is the treasure chest of the world—the public library or a bookstore."
◎ "Successful people don't have fewer problems. They have determined that nothing will stop them from going forward."
◎ "Knowledge is the key that unlocks all the doors. You can be green-skinned with yellow polka dots and come from Mars, but if you have knowledge that people need, instead of beating you, they'll beat a path to your door."
◎ "I am convinced that knowledge is power—to overcome the past, to change our own situations, to fight new obstacles, to make better decisions."
◎ "If you look at these obstacles as a containing fence, they become your excuses for failure. If you look at them as a hurdle, each one strengthens you for the next."
◎ "Happiness doesn't result from what we get, but from what we give."
◎ "I tackle things that other people won't tackle. . . . It simply has to do with me asking the question: 'What's the best thing and what's the worst that happens if I do something, what's the best thing and what's the worst

thing that happens if I do nothing?' On the basis of those four questions, I can determine whether I should do something or not."

◎ "Our Creator has endowed all of us not just with the ability to sing, dance or throw a ball, but with intellectual talent. Start getting in touch with that part of you that is intellectual and develop that, and think of careers that will allow you to use that."

◎ "If you lead a clean and honest life, you don't put skeletons in the closet. If you put skeletons in the closet, they definitely will come back just when you don't want to see them and ruin your life."

◎ "Insight: It comes from people who have already gone where you're trying to go. Learn from their triumphs and their mistakes."

◎ "If you're nice to people, then once they get over the suspicion of why you're being nice, they will be nice to you."

◎ "Knowledge: It makes you into a more valuable person. The more knowledge you have, the more people need you. It's an interesting phenomenon, but when people need you, they pay you, so you'll be okay in life."

◎ "Learn for the sake of knowledge and understanding, rather than for the sake of impressing people or taking a test."

Awards and Recognition

◎ 2008: Awarded the Presidential Medal of Freedom
◎ Has at least 61 honorary doctorates
◎ Member of the American Academy of Achievement
◎ Sits on the board of directors for several national corporations and charities
◎ Recipient of the Ford's Theatre Lincoln Medal and William E. Simon Prize for Philanthropic Leadership
◎ 2010: Elected to the Institute of Medicine of the United States National Academy of Sciences

Lasting Impact and Contributions

◎ Pioneered innovations in brain surgery that extended the capability of the field to remediate debilitating conditions
◎ Serves as a powerful role model for youth, especially those from disadvantaged backgrounds and single-parent households
◎ Strong advocate for achievement through diligence and hard work with no excuses
◎ Originator of a scholarship fund to encourage educational excellence and service

Teachers' Rap Sheet

Amelia Earhart

Full Name: Amelia Mary Earhart

Lifespan: July 24, 1897–July 2, 1937 (the day she disappeared; declared dead in absentia in January 1939)

Early Family Background and Created Family Structure

- ◎ Born in Atchison, KS
- ◎ Named after two grandmothers; nicknamed Meeley or Millie
- ◎ Grandfather was a federal judge and then president of a local bank; father was a lawyer and employed by Rock Island Railroad
- ◎ Had one sister, Grace Muriel (Midge), 2 years younger
- ◎ Family moved to Des Moines, IA, when she was 9 for her father's job
- ◎ Age 10: She went to the Iowa State Fair and saw her first plane, but she could not be convinced to take a ride in it
- ◎ Family was economically comfortable, but her father's battle with alcohol forced him into early retirement; her mother inherited a trust fund from her mother's estate
- ◎ 1915: Mother moved girls to Chicago when her father couldn't find a position
- ◎ 1924: Her parents separated; her disappointment with her father made it difficult for her to put her trust in men
- ◎ 1931: Married George P. Putnam, who proposed to her six times before she finally accepted
- ◎ Had no children of her own, but had two stepsons (David and George) from her husband's first marriage

Education

- ◎ Mother raised children to be free spirits, not conforming children
- ◎ Homeschooled by mother and a governess until age 12 when she entered seventh grade at public school in Des Moines
- ◎ 1916: Graduated from Hyde Park High School in Chicago where she was enrolled because of its excellent science program
- ◎ 1916: Entered Ogontz, a girl's finishing school in Rydal, PA, but did not finish
- ◎ 1917: Received training as nurse's aide from the Red Cross
- ◎ 1919: Enrolled at Columbia University for a year in medical studies

Personality Characteristics and Areas of Aptitude, Talent, and Interest

◎ Daredevil who had a strong spirit of adventure as a child; liked to play outdoors and was characterized as a tomboy
◎ Was seen as drab and lonely in her high school yearbook
◎ Courageous and selfless; she came in third in her first racing competition because she delayed her take-off to assist another competitor whose plane had crashed
◎ Was fiercely independent, persistent, and cool under pressure
◎ Extremely private person who used the public eye to advance her love of flying and her commitment to equal rights for women
◎ Age 7: Attached a homemade ramp to the garage and slid off in a wooden box that served as a sled; although bruised and disheveled, she remarked to her sister that it was "just like flying"
◎ Amateur poet who published one poem titled "Courage" (most of her poems were destroyed in a house fire)
◎ 1920: Visited an airfield where she was given her first airplane ride and found it exhilarating

Major Career/Professional Events and Accomplishments

◎ 1917: Began work as a nurse's aide at Spadina Military Hospital in Toronto, Canada
◎ 1920: Worked a variety of jobs to save $1,000 for flying lessons and received her first lesson on January 3, 1921 in California from a pioneer female aviator; had to take a bus and walk 4 miles to the airfield
◎ 1922: Purchased her first plane, a bright yellow, used Kinner Airster biplane that she nicknamed the Canary; set a world record for reaching an altitude of 14,000 feet by a female pilot on October 22 of that year
◎ 1925: Amelia and her mother moved to Massachusetts where she worked as a teacher and social worker and stayed connected to flying by joining the Boston chapter of the American Aeronautical Society; flew the first flight out of Dennison Airport in 1927 and wrote columns for the local newspaper promoting flying
◎ 1928: Entered first all-women air race nicknamed the Powder Puff Derby by Will Rogers
◎ June 17, 1928: First woman to fly across the Atlantic (as a passenger and log keeper), a project coordinated by publisher George Putnam (who became her husband); greeted with a ticker tape parade when she and her cohorts returned to New York
◎ Undertook a lecture tour and authored a book; notoriety led to endorsement for luggage, clothing, and cigarette ads
◎ 1928: Became the first woman to fly solo across the North American continent and back

◎ 1929: One of the first aviators to promote commercial air travel and involved in the establishment of proprietary airline ventures that led to the formation of TWA and Northeast Airlines

◎ 1930: Became a charter member and first president of The Ninety-Nines, an organization of women pilots that crusaded for women's rights in the field of aviation

◎ 1931: Set world altitude record of 18,415 feet

◎ May 20–21, 1932: Became the first aviatrix to fly solo across the Atlantic (from Newfoundland to Culmore, Northern Ireland)

◎ First woman to fly across the Atlantic twice

◎ 1935: Became the first person to fly solo from Honolulu, HI, to Oakland, CA

◎ Between 1930 and 1935, she set seven women's speed and distance aviation records

◎ 1935: Earhart partnered with Paul Mantz to start a short-lived flying school in California; her husband was working for one of the Hollywood studios at the time

◎ 1935: Joined the faculty of Purdue University as a visiting lecturer to advise women on careers in aeronautics and also advised the Department of Aeronautics

◎ June 1, 1937: Departed Miami, FL, for her second attempt to circumnavigate the globe; Earhart and her navigator, Fred Noonan, arrived at Lae, New Guinea on June 29, completing about 22,000 of the planned 29,000-mile route

◎ July 2, 1937: Took off for Howland Island with Noonan, but disappeared

◎ Land and sea search for her plane were most costly and intensive in U.S. history ($4 million)

◎ Wrote three books: *20 Hrs., 40 Min.: Our Flight in the Friendship*; *The Fun of It*; and *Last Flight* (compiled by her husband after her disappearance)

Personal Life Themes/Beliefs

◎ Marriage is a partnership with "dual controls" and openness
◎ Men and women are equal in skills, aptitudes, and abilities
◎ Fatalistic, with carpe diem philosophy

Selected Quotations

◎ "Never interrupt someone doing what you said couldn't be done."
◎ "The most effective way to do it, is to do it."
◎ "I want to do something useful in the world."
◎ "Women must pay for everything. They do get more glory than men for comparable feats. But, they also get more notoriety when they crash."

◎ "In soloing—as in other activities—it is far easier to start something than it is to finish it."

◎ "The most difficult thing is the decision to act, the rest is merely tenacity. The fears are paper tigers. You can do anything you decide to do. You can act to change and control your life; and the procedures, the process is its own reward."

◎ "A single act of kindness throws out roots in all directions, and the roots spring up and make new trees. The greatest work that kindness does to others is that it makes them kind themselves."

Awards and Recognition

◎ 1932: First woman to receive the U.S. Distinguished Flying Cross from U.S. Congress

◎ 1932: Received the Cross of Knight from the Legion of Honor from France

◎ 132: Received the Gold Medal from the National Geographic Society

◎ Had scholarships established in her name, airports named after her, and a birthplace museum opened in her honor in her hometown

◎ A biopic titled *Amelia* was released in 2009, starring Hilary Swank

Lasting Impact and Contributions

◎ Known as one of world's most celebrated aviators and regarded as a feminist icon

◎ Inspired a generation of women flyers including the WASPs (Women Air Force Service Pilots) of World War II

◎ Symbolized hope for a brighter future during the Depression

Teachers' Rap Sheet
Bill Gates

Full Name: William (Bill) Henry Gates, III

Lifespan: October 28, 1955 to present

Early Family Background and Created Family Structure

- Born in Seattle, WA
- Father was a prominent lawyer; mother served on the board of directors of an interstate bank and the United Way
- Maternal grandfather was a national bank president
- Has one elder and one younger sister
- 1994: Married Melinda French
- Has two daughters and one son

Education

- Age 13: Enrolled in Lakeside School
- 1973: Graduated from Lakeside School
- 1973: Served as Congressional page in the U.S. House of Representatives
- 1973: Enrolled at Harvard University
- Dropped out of Harvard as a sophomore to start his own computer software company

Personality Characteristics and Areas of Aptitude, Talent, and Interest

- Had a reputation for being the brightest child in school, especially in math and science
- Often got bored and landed in trouble
- Finished math tests early and filled pages with detailed essays on scientific subjects
- Was teased for doing well and would sometimes deliberately get lower grades
- Belonged to the Boy Scouts rather than sports teams
- Good at understanding details and catching onto things quickly
- Can integrate things into a big-picture view in real time
- Distant and often did not return phone calls
- Verbally combative
- Avid reader whose favorite book is *Catcher in the Rye*
- Started a programmer's group while at Lakeside School that took on projects for local businesses, such as calculating time sheets and vacation and sick leave usage

◎ Wrote the computer program at Lakeside School to schedule students in classes

◎ Excused from math classes in high school to pursue an interest in programming

◎ Scored 1590 out of 1600 on SAT for college admission

◎ In college, he devised an algorithm that he and a Harvard computer scientist published

◎ Enjoys playing bridge, tennis, and golf

Major Career/Professional Events and Accomplishments

◎ Active software developer in his early years and manager and executive in later years

◎ 1976: Started Microsoft and is best known as its founder

◎ 1980: Developed MS-DOS for IBM and other vendors

◎ 1981: Launched Microsoft Windows

◎ 1981: Became President and Chairman of the Board and maintained primary responsibility for product strategy until 2006

◎ 1987: Declared a billionaire at age 32 (worth $1.25 billion)

◎ 1989: Founded Corbis, a digital imaging company

◎ 1994: Created the William H. Gates Foundation

◎ 2000: Established the Bill and Melinda Gates Foundation, the largest foundation in the world

◎ 2004: Became a director of Berkshire Hathaway

◎ 2006: Stepped down from a day-to-day role at Microsoft to devote more time to philanthropy

◎ Modeled his philanthropic ideas after the Rockefellers by focusing on global problems often ignored by other organizations

◎ Charitable initiatives have focused on global health issues, especially malaria and AIDS in poor countries, and education

Personal Life Themes/Beliefs

◎ Agnostic raised as a Congregationalist

◎ Belief in doing good in the world

◎ Espouses the importance of giving back (inherited from his mother)

Selected Quotations

◎ "There was just something neat about the machine" (reflecting back on his eighth-grade experience with computers).

◎ "It was hard to tear myself away from a machine at which I could so unambiguously demonstrate success."

◎ "I'll do it over the weekend" (in response to subordinates' procrastination).

◎ "Maybe I'd have been more rounded if there weren't as many books around."

◎ "Many problems in society are just poorly designed algorithms."

◎ "Often you have to rely on intuition."

◎ "We all learn best in our own ways. Some people do better studying one subject at a time, while some do better studying three things at once. Some people do best studying in structured, linear way, while others do best jumping around, 'surrounding' a subject rather than traversing it. Some people prefer to learn by manipulating models, and others by reading."

◎ "There's no year that I didn't love my job."

◎ "I was fortunate to have family and teachers who encouraged me. Children often thrive when they get that kind of attention."

◎ "I guess you could call me the doer and Paul [Allen] the ideas man. I'm more aggressive and crazily competitive."

◎ "I believe that if you show people the problems, and you show them the solutions, they will be moved to act."

◎ "As we look ahead into the next century, leaders will be those who empower others."

◎ "At Microsoft there are lots of brilliant ideas, but the image is that they come from the top—I'm afraid that's not quite right."

◎ "Be nice to nerds. Chances are you'll end up working for one."

◎ "I think it's fair to say that personal computers have become the most empowering tool we've ever created. They're tools of communication; they're tools of creativity, and they can be shaped by their user."

Awards and Recognition

◎ Has received multiple honorary doctorates

◎ 1994: Became 20th Distinguished Fellow of British Computer Society

◎ 2004, 2005, and 2006: Named by *TIME* magazine as one of the top 100 people of the century

◎ 2010: Received the Bower award for business leadership and philanthropy

◎ 2011: Ranked as the fifth most powerful person in world according to *Forbes* magazine

◎ Had a fly named in his honor by an entomologist

Lasting Impact and Contributions

◎ Pioneer and visionary in the field of computer technology

◎ Spearheaded a technological shift that led to utilization of computers by huge segments of society

◎ Notable philanthropist who focuses on global rather than just national problems

Teachers' Rap Sheet

Clara Barton

Full Name: Clarissa Harlowe Barton

Life Span: December 25, 1821–April 12, 1912

Early Family Background and Created Family Structure

- Was born the youngest of five children
- Cared for by older sisters, one of whom had a mental breakdown when Clara was 6
- Came from a family with a history of mental illness
- Father served in the Revolutionary War and the American Indian Wars, and his stories familiarized Clara with war from a young age
- Began nursing her brother at the age of 11, after his injury in a construction accident
- Never married

Education

- Began school at 4 years old, not an uncommon age at the time
- Taught by her older siblings, she later said she could not recall a time when she couldn't read
- Received sporadic formal schooling throughout childhood; began her own teaching career at nearby schools as a teenager
- Studied for a year at the Clinton Liberal Institute in Clinton, NY, at the age of 30

Personality Characteristics and Areas of Aptitude, Talent, and Interest

- Was extremely shy; began teaching on the advice of a phrenologist as an attempt to combat shyness
- Displayed sympathy and devotion to caring for others
- Battled lifelong depression and a lack of confidence in her personal worth
- Was tough and perseverant

Major Career/Professional Events and Accomplishments

- Founded first free school in New Jersey, raising enrollment from six students to more than 200; left after she was passed over for an administrative spot in favor of a man
- Worked in Washington as first female clerk in the Patent Office

◎ 1861: Cared for the Sixth Massachusetts troops after they arrived in Washington, nursing the seriously wounded in her sister's home because the city had no facilities

◎ Provided relief services to the wounded at many Civil War battle sites

◎ 1865–1867: Operated the Office of Correspondence with Friends of the Missing Men of the United States Army out of her Capitol Hill apartment, identifying more than 22,000 missing soldiers

◎ Helped create a national cemetery around the graves of Union men who died at the infamous Andersonville prison

◎ Became a household name through her 2-year speaking tour with the lecture "Work and Incidents of Army Life"

◎ Worked for the International Red Cross in war-torn France during the Franco-Prussian War

◎ 1881: Founded the American Red Cross after realizing the model could be useful for civilian disasters as well as wartime relief

◎ 1882: Influenced the United States to sign the Geneva Treaty

Personal Life Themes/Beliefs

◎ Her father was active in the local Universalist church, which Clara attended with her family throughout her childhood

◎ Developed an interest in spiritualism and Christian Science later in life, but she never joined a church

◎ Experienced joy in suffering personal discomforts and privations in the service of others

◎ Had two governing principles of action: "unconcern for what cannot be helped" and "control under pressure"

Selected Quotations

◎ "I have an almost complete disregard of precedent, and a faith in the possibility of something better. It irritates me to be told how things have always been done. I defy the tyranny of precedent. I go for anything new that might improve the past."

◎ "The door that nobody else will go in at, seems always to swing open widely for me."

◎ "I may be compelled to face danger, but never fear it, and while our soldiers can stand and fight, I can stand and feed and nurse them."

◎ "I always tried . . . to succor the wounded until medical aid and supplies could come up. I could run the risk; it made no difference to anyone if I were shot or taken prisoner."

◎ "An institution or reform movement that is not selfish, must originate in the recognition of some evil that is adding to the sum of human suffering, or diminishing the sum of happiness."

◎ "The surest test of discipline is its absence."

◎ "I may sometimes be willing to teach for nothing, but if paid at all, I shall never do a man's work for less than a man's pay."

◎ "It has long been said, that women don't know anything about war. I wish men didn't either. They have always known a great deal too much about it for the good of their kind."

◎ "To this day, I would rather stand behind the lines of artillery at Antietam or cross the pontoon bridge under fire at Fredericksburg, than to be expected to preside at a public meeting."

Awards and Recognition

◎ Most decorated American woman, receiving the German Iron Cross, the Silver Cross of Imperial Russia, and the International Red Cross Medal

◎ Inducted into the National Women's Hall of Fame in Seneca Falls, NY, in 1973

◎ 1975: Clara Barton National Historic Site established as a unit of the National Park Service at her Glen Echo, MD, home, the first National Historic Site dedicated to the accomplishments of a woman

Lasting Impact and Contributions

◎ Founded the American Red Cross, which is one of the largest humanitarian organizations in the world

◎ Her legacy opened new doors for civilians to assist in disaster relief efforts and continues to inspire medical professionals today

Teachers' Rap Sheet
Tecumseh

Full Name: Tecumseh

Life Span: ca. 1768–October 5, 1813

Early Family Background and Created Family Structure

◎ Born into the Shawnee tribe
◎ Father Puckshinwa fought against the Americans in the Revolutionary War
◎ 1774: Father "brutally murdered" when Tecumseh was a boy by White frontiersmen who had crossed onto Indian land in violation of a recent treaty
◎ Resolved to become a warrior like his father and be "a fire spreading over the hill and valley, consuming the race of dark souls"
◎ At least five times during his childhood, Tecumseh's village was attacked by colonials and later American armies because the Shawnees had allied with the British during the Revolutionary War

Personality Characteristics and Areas of Aptitude, Talent, and Interest

◎ Was very courageous
◎ Had remarkable eloquence as an orator
◎ Had great intelligence and learning; studied the Bible and world history

Major Career/Professional Events and Accomplishments

◎ 1790s: Participated in major battles with White settlers over the Ohio country
◎ Used his brother Tenskwatawa ("the Prophet")'s millenarian religious teachings to found a political movement based on trans-Indian unity and retention of land
◎ Marshaled more than 1,000 Native Americans to fight with Great Britain against the United States in the War of 1812
◎ Stopped his soldiers from slaughtering prisoners of war
◎ Continued fighting for tribal land even after the retreat of the British left 500 Native Americans pitted against 3,000 Whites; died in battle

Personal Life Themes/Beliefs

◎ Belief in the Great Spirit and the traditional Indian way of life
◎ Fervent opposition to the practice of treating land as property

◎ Commitment to united intertribal federation to stand against the United States' seizure of land

Selected Quotations

◎ "The Great Spirit above has appointed this place for us, on which to light our fires, and here we will remain. As to boundaries, the Great Spirit above knows no boundaries, nor will his red people acknowledge any."

◎ "Sell a country? Why not sell the air, the great sea, as well as the earth? Didn't the Great Spirit make them all for the use of his children?"

◎ "The only way to stop this evil is for the red man to unite in claiming a common and equal right in the land, as it was first, and should be now, for it was never divided."

◎ "The whites are already nearly a match for us all united, and too strong for any one tribe alone to resist. Unless we support one another with our collective forces, they will soon conquer us, and we will be driven away from our native country and scattered as leaves before the wind."

◎ "We are determined to defend our lands and, if it be the Great Spirit's will, we wish to leave our bones upon them."

Awards and Recognition

◎ Had various statues in the Midwest and Canada erected in his honor

◎ Head has been featured on coins

◎ Honored in Canada as a hero who played a major role in Canada's successful repulsion of an American invasion during the War of 1812

◎ A number of battleships and towns, as well as Civil War general Tecumseh Sherman, were named after him

Lasting Impact and Contributions

◎ Left a legacy as a war hero and symbol of Native American resistance to oppression

◎ Inspired many works of poetry, novels, and art

Appendix B
Annotated Bibliography

Biographic Compendia

Adams, S., Ashe, C., Chrisp, P., Johnson, E., Langley, A., & Weeks, M. (1999). *1000 makers of the millennium.* New York, NY: DK Publishing.

Organized into 10 centuries, the book identifies and provides brief biographies of 1,000 influential people. Many color photographs and illustrations are included. There is a strong contingent of celebrities and sports figures chosen for the late 1900s, which may be a commentary on the times in which we live.

Ashby, R., & Ohrn, D. G. (Eds.). (1995). *Herstory: Women who changed the world.* New York, NY: Viking Press.

This reference book begins with an introductory essay by Gloria Steinem that documents several examples of prejudice against women up through the last half of the 20th century. The book is subdivided into three sections, grouped by time periods: prehistory to 1750; 1750 to 1850; and 1890 to around 1990. The first section contains 21 brief biographies, including Queen Hatshepsut, Sappho, Joan of Arc, Queen Isabella I, and Queen Elizabeth I. Section II contains more than 40 brief biographies including Sacajawea, Sojourner Truth, the Brontë sisters, Clara Barton, Jane Addams, and Beatrix Potter. The third section contains more than 50 brief biographies of women from a wide range of fields. All three sections have introductory essays and are drawn from an international template.

Meadows, J. (1997). *The world's great minds.* London, England: Chancellor Press.

Biographies of 12 great thinkers are presented with supporting information about the times and cultures in which their contributions were embedded. The individuals include Aristotle, Galileo Galilei, William Harvey, Sir Isaac Newton, Antoine Lavoisier, Alexander von Humboldt, Michael Faraday, Charles Darwin, Louis Pasteur, Marie Curie, Sigmund Freud, and Albert Einstein. This text contains many color and black and white photographs and illustrations.

The Editors of Salem Press. (2009). *American heroes* (Vol. 3). Pasadena, CA: The Salem Press.

Sixty-four brief biographies with reference citations are presented alphabetically for American notables whose last names range from Nicklaus to Zacharias. Included are such luminaries as Chester Nimitz, Sandra Day O'Connor, Walter Reed, Jackie Robinson, Eleanor Roosevelt, Sacajawea, and Tecumseh. There are two other volumes of this book that contain brief biographies of leaders included in this curriculum unit. Volume 1 covers heroes whose names range from Aaron to Geronimo. Included in this volume are Jane Addams, Robert Ballard, Clara Barton, Rachel Carson, Cesar Chavez, Walt Disney, Amelia Earhart, Dwight Eisenhower, and Bill Gates. Volume 2 ranges from Gibson to Navratilova and includes Steve Jobs.

Time/CBS News. (1999). *People of the century: One hundred men and women who shaped the last one hundred years*. New York, NY: Simon and Schuster.

Biographical information in the context of brief essays is presented on 100 personalities or representatives of ideas that media sources suggested define the 20th century. The people selected range from Sigmund Freud, Emmeline Pankhurst, Theodore Roosevelt, and Henry Ford at the beginning of the 1900s, to Oprah Winfrey, Bill Gates, Bart Simpson, and the "Unknown Tiananmen Square Rebel" at the end of the century. Interesting photographs in both color and black and white are interspersed with the text.

Juvenile Biographies on Leaders in Unit

The following biographies have been selected as reading material for the leaders studied in this unit because they are age-appropriate and provide important biographical information in a well-written and entertaining way. In some cases, the reading level may not be particularly challenging for some readers, but no other texts were available for consideration at the juvenile level that offered more advanced reading levels.

Fleming, C. (2011). *Amelia lost: The life and disappearance of Amelia Earhart*. New York, NY: Schwartz and Wade. (For ages 8 and up)

Greene, K., & Greene, R. (1998). *The man behind the magic: The story of Walt Disney*. New York, NY: Viking Juvenile. (For grades 6–12)

Krensky, S. (2011). *DK biography: Clara Barton*. New York, NY: DK Children. (For ages 9 and up)

Lesinski, J. M. (2007). *Bill Gates*. Minneapolis, MN: Lerner. (For ages 10 and up)

Lesinski, J. M. (2009). *Bill Gates: Entrepreneur and philanthropist*. Minneapolis, MN: Lerner. (For ages 11 and up)

Lewis, G., & Lewis, D. S. (2009). *Gifted hands, kids edition: The Ben Carson story*. Grand Rapids, MI: ZonderKidz. (For ages 9 and up)

Zimmerman, D. J. (2010). *Tecumseh: Shooting star of the Shawnee*. New York, NY: Sterling Press. (For ages 10 and up)

Research Literature on Leadership

Bennis, W., & Goldsmith, J. (2010). *Learning to lead: A workbook on becoming a leader* (4th ed.). New York, NY: Basic Books.

This text identifies four characteristics that are wanted from today's leaders (providing purpose, direction, and meaning; building and sustaining trust; purveying hope and optimism; and delivering results) and offers insights and explication to help managers develop into leaders.

Blank, W. (2001). *The 108 skills of natural born leaders*. New York, NY: Amacom.

Starting with the premise that no one is a born leader, this text identifies 108 skills that can be developed to strengthen leadership capabilities in people. Blank differentiates between people who are managers and people who are leaders. He includes a self-assessment inventory that organizes the 108 skills into nine sets: self-awareness, capacity to develop rapport with people, ability to clarify expectations, ability to map the territory to identify the need to lead, ability to chart a course of leadership action, ability to develop others as leaders, ability to build the base to gain commitment, ability to influence others to willingly follow, and ability to create a motivating environment. The last skill he posits is the ability to continually seek renewal.

Bolman, L. G., & Deal, T. E. (2008). *Reframing organizations: Artistry, choice, and leadership* (4th ed.). San Francisco, CA: Jossey-Bass.

The authors offer an interesting lens through which to view the leadership construct. They suggest that effective leadership involves making judgments about the combined use of four leadership frames: (1) structural—the role of tasks and organizational hierarchies (architect); (2) human resources—the role of relationship building (catalyst); (3) political—the role of power distribution (advocate); and (4) symbolic—the role of meaning (prophet). They see leadership as situational and change as involving conflict and loss. Their perspective is drawn from the field of business, and they identify the characteristics of high-performing companies.

Covey, S. R. (2004). *The 7 habits of highly effective people* (Rev. ed.). New York, NY: Simon and Schuster.

This bestseller identifies seven time-honored factors that underscore effective leadership. Covey's synthesis includes (1) being proactive, honoring commitments, and initiating change; (2) developing personal mission statements, setting goals, and identifying desired outcomes; (3) the importance of self-awareness and identity; (4) prioritizing what's important (planning, organizing, time management); (5) win-win relationship-building (character, integrity, trust, cooperation, and honesty); (6) empathic communication (listening and understanding); and (7) creative cooperation (synergy), team-building, and collaboration.

Gardner, H. (2011). *Creating minds: An anatomy of creativity seen through the lives of Freud, Einstein, Picasso, Stravinsky, Eliot, Graham, and Gandhi.* New York, NY: Basic Books.

The author uses the study of seven creative individuals drawn from different domains to offer insights on the construct of creativity. He believes that creativity evolves from the interaction of domains, individuals, and fields and that it is novel problem solving within a domain that ultimately becomes accepted. He discusses the criticality of early support and the Faustian bargain that individuals make in order to rise to the top of their fields.

Hamer, D., & Copeland, P. (1998). *Living with our genes: Why they matter more than you think.* New York, NY: Doubleday Books.

Behavioral aptitudes, personality preferences, and individual temperaments are programmed into our genes, but preference does not mean that the behavior will be actualized. True skill mastery requires practice. This understanding of the developmental dimension of leadership underscores the lessons in this curriculum unit.

Kouzes, J. M., & Posner, B. Z. (1999). *The leadership challenge planner: An action guide to achieving your personal best.* San Francisco, CA: Jossey-Bass.

This clear and insightful text identifies five skill sets that define effective leadership. The authors posit that leaders (1) are pioneers and early adopters of innovation who lead the way by challenging the process and taking risks, (2) inspire a shared vision through dialogue, (3) enable others to act through team-building, (4) model the way through careful planning, and (5) encourage and nurture by feedback, praise, celebration, and rewards.

Mai, R., & Akerson, A. (2003). *The leader as communicator: Strategies and tactics to build loyalty, focus effort, and spark creativity.* New York, NY: Amacom.

This text makes the argument that the primary skill set in effective leadership is related to communication and that leadership communication is about relationship building. It identifies three communication roles for leaders: building community by making meaning, navigating and setting direction, and championing the renewal process. The chapter entitled "Storyteller" relates how the use of stories, anecdotes, and parables can inform and educate as well as inspire.

Nanus, B. (1992). *Visionary leadership.* San Francisco, CA: Jossey-Bass.

This primer on leadership endorses the idea that there are differences between managers and leaders (previously posited by Bennis and Goldsmith) and discusses specific characteristics related to the idea of vision, including that a powerful vision is capable of attracting others, creating meaning, establishing excellence, and forecasting future directions. The author believes that leadership is a mix of judgment (structure, assessment, form, and purpose) and instinct (intuition) and that teaching leadership is important at K–12 levels if the U.S. is to be competitive in the 21st century.

Payne, V. (2001). *The team-building workshop.* New York, NY: Amacom.

This text offers steps, strategies, and exercises in the art of team-building, starting with an understanding of the value of team-building to an organization. It is designed for individuals who are conducting team-building workshops or sessions. Of particular note is the section on resolving team conflict and the inventory of experiential exercises.

Quick, T. L. (1992). *Successful team building.* New York, NY: Amacom.

This how-to manual for team-building offers helpful chapters on the nature and benefits of a team, including characteristics of effective and ineffective teams, building commitment, dealing with conflict, and group problem solving and decision making.

Simonton, D. K. (1994). *Greatness: Who makes history and why.* New York, NY: Guilford Press.

Using historical research as a basis for exploring the concept of greatness, Simonton offers valuable insights that impact the literature on the construct of leadership. Among the ideas he explores are the role of creativity in leadership; human potential and the development of talent (born or learned or situational); the role of models and mentors in leadership; the importance of personality (self-actualizers, extroversion and introversion); early exposure and learning in a field as predictive of later accomplishment; factors of family, education, stimulation, adversity, and marginality; and the role of motivation and drive.

Wallace, D. B., & Gruber, H. E. (1989). *Creative people at work: Twelve cognitive case studies.* New York, NY: Oxford University Press.

This interesting take on creativity discusses ideas that have salience for the research on leadership. The text is organized around four basic themes: (1) an evolving systems approach (organization of knowledge, purpose, and affect) to understanding the construct of creativity in the domain of work, (2) networks of enterprise, (3) the role of novelty and chance, and (4) personal freedom and social responsibility—the twin tensions of creators/leaders (i.e., moral and ethical leadership).

About the Authors

Joyce VanTassel-Baska, Ed.D., is the Jody and Layton Smith Professor Emerita at The College of William and Mary, where she developed a graduate program and a research and development center in gifted education. Formerly, she initiated and directed the Center for Talent Development at Northwestern University. She has also served as the state director of gifted programs for Illinois, as a regional director of a gifted service center in the Chicago area, as coordinator of gifted programs for the Toledo, OH, public school system, and as a teacher of gifted high school students in English and Latin. Dr. VanTassel-Baska has published widely, including 27 books and more than 500 refereed journal articles, book chapters, and scholarly reports. Her major research interests are the talent development process and effective curricular interventions with the gifted.

Linda D. Avery, Ph.D., managed the Center for Gifted Education at The College of William and Mary upon receiving her doctorate in educational leadership, policy, and planning from that institution in the late 1990s. Previously she helped establish the first gifted education program at the state level in Michigan and helped administer the long-established state program in Illinois. She has authored language arts curriculum materials based on the Integrated Curriculum Model (ICM) and oversaw the preparation of a collection of social studies curriculum units. She has conducted several state and local gifted program evaluation studies over her career and numerous professional development workshops in curriculum development and implementation. She is currently living in Seville, OH.